Ohio Bucket List Adventure Guide

*Explore 100 Offbeat
Destinations You Must Visit!*

Cynthia Brandt

Canyon Press
canyon@purplelink.org

Please consider writing a review!
Just visit: purplelink.org/review

ISBN: 978-1-957590-09-7

FREE BONUS

Discover 31 Incredible Places You Can
Visit Next! Just Go To:

purplelink.org/travel

Table of Contents:

How to Use This Book

Welcome to your very own adventure guide to exploring the many wonders of the state of Ohio. Not only does this book offer the most wonderful places to visit and sights to see in the vast state, but it provides GPS coordinates for Google Maps to make exploring that much easier.

Adventure Guide
Sorted by region, this guide offers over 100 amazing wonders found in Ohio for you to see and explore. They can be visited in any order, and this book will help you keep track of where you've been and where to look forward to going next. Each section describes the area or place, what to look for, Physical Address, and what you may need to bring along.

GPS Coordinates
As you can imagine, not all of the locations in this book have a physical address. Fortunately, some of our listed wonders are either located within a National Park or Reserve or near a city, town, or place of business. For those that are not associated with a specific location, it is easiest to map it using GPS coordinates.

Luckily, Google has a system of codes that converts the coordinates into pin-drop locations that Google Maps can interpret and navigate.

Each adventure in this guide includes GPS coordinates along with a physical address whenever it is available.

It is important that you are prepared for poor cell signals. It is recommended that you route your location and ensure that the directions are accessible offline. Depending on your device and the distance of some locations, you may need to travel with a backup battery source.

About Ohio

Over 400 million years ago, Ice Age glaciers cut their way through the Ohio River Valley, carving out the Great Lakes and leaving behind miles and miles of uncovered sandstone and marine fossils for modern-day visitors to find. The unique collection of gorges, cliffs, caves, and glacial grooves cannot be found anywhere else in the country, and the Buckeye Hiking Trail that covers the entire state gives visitors access to every one of these natural phenomena.

Whether you're planning a weekend getaway or a weeks-long backpacking hike, Ohio is a place to see all year round. Campgrounds are open from January through December, and winter activities at most state parks include dog sledding, ice fishing, snowmobiling, hiking, and cross-country skiing. Most of the waterfalls discussed in this book are at their most beautiful after they ice over for the winter, and they are a sight to see when crowds of summer tourists aren't filling up the trails.

However, summer remains the best time to swim and explore the shores of Lake Erie. Each beach offers different accommodations, from concession stands and live music to jet skis. Not every part of the lake allows engines, but where they do, visitors can bring up to 399 horsepower for tubing, wakeboarding, and water skiing.

Ohio remains one of the few states with free access to state parks and nature preserves. Hiking and biking trails, fishing, and swimming are free at most spots discussed in this book, and campsite reservations can start as low as $5 per night for primitive and non-electric hookups. This means it is completely free to explore some of the most unique ecosystems and geological formations in the country.

Landscape and Climate

Ohio's landscape ranges from ancient plains to sandy beaches to sky-high cliffs thanks to its proximity to the Great Lakes. Visitors can soak up the sun along the shores of Lake Erie or get lost in the deep woods of ancient oaks and hemlocks. Elevation changes during your hikes can be steep and sudden due to the ancient glacial activity, but the weather remains rather temperate from spring to fall.

Numerous state parks throughout Ohio showcase the different landscapes of the state, which include the Great Lakes Plains, the Appalachian Plateau, the Bluegrass Region, the Lake Erie shoreline, and the Tills Plains, which were carved by glaciers during the Ice Age.

There are many unique rock formations to explore in Ohio because of the glacial activity in this area over 400 million years ago. Natural bridges and rock arches are among the most common, including the Rock House, with an arch of 40 feet, and the Rockbridge Arch that spans 100 feet long. For a truly unique sight, visit the Needle's Eye, which is a marine arch located on the shores of Lake Erie.

Visiting Ohio is your chance to experience all four seasons as there are distinct differences that you don't always see in other Midwestern states. The lake is to blame for the seasonal variability.

Overall, the climate remains humid throughout the year, with the chance for lake-effect snowstorms relatively high on the southern coast of Lake Erie. This area is aptly known as "the Snowbelt," and you may experience snow squalls and up to 60 inches of snow and ice in the winter.

Great Blue Heron Viewing Area

Great blue herons are impressive birds that are 4 feet tall with 7-foot wingspans. They are in peak plumage from February through June during their breeding season. Visitors to Great Blue Heron Viewing Area, also known as Bath Road Heronry, a nesting colony, can watch them performing courtship displays, repairing nests, and raising their young high above the passing cars.

A paved pullout with a wayside exhibit along Bath Road, just east of the Cuyahoga River, is an ideal place for viewing. The herons are behind a fence on the south side of the road on the property of the Akron Water Reclamation Facility. They typically build their nests in trees from 30 to 70 feet high and surrounded by water.

Best Time to Visit: You'll see mating displays when you visit in June.

Pass/Permit/Fees: It's free to birdwatch on Blue Road.

Closest City or Town: Akron

Physical Address: 3801 Riverview Rd, Peninsula, OH 44264

GPS Coordinates: 41.1634° N, 81.5707° W

Did You Know? Male and female herons share in nest building and caring for the young.

Goodyear Airdock

This was once a center for the construction of dirigibles. Two lighter-than-air blimps were constructed here—the *Akron* ZRS-4 and the *Macon* ZRS-5—and launched in 1931 and 1934, respectively. When completed in 1929, it was the largest building in the world. But dirigibles didn't last long, and the Airdock became host to rallies, speeches, and other forms of military–aerospace construction.

The Goodyear Airdock is currently owned by the Lockheed Martin Corporation and is not open to the public, but you can photograph the exterior from Emmitt Road.

Best Time to Visit: Drive by for a photo-op between April and September when the weather is less likely to obstruct the view.

Pass/Permit/Fees: It's free to see the airdock from Exeter Road or Emmitt Road.

Closest City or Town: Akron

Physical Address: 1210 Massillon Rd, Akron, OH 44315

GPS Coordinates: 41.0319° N, 81.4708° W

Did You Know? President Bill Clinton gave one of his campaign speeches at the Goodyear Airdock in 1992.

Resting Place of the Giants

One of the quirkiest facts about Ohio is that it's the resting place of the world's tallest married couple. Captain Martin Van Buren Bates and his wife Anna Swan Bates were both over 7 feet tall. Anna stood at 7'11". The couple traveled with P.T. Barnum's Museum and toured much of the globe before settling in Ohio, but their wishes to start a family never came true. Anna gave birth to two children, a daughter, and a son, but both died in infancy.

The couple is buried in Cy-Hewitt Mound Hill Cemetery, and their graves are marked by the statue of a tall woman on a pedestal. Their infant son, who was born at a record-breaking 30 inches long, is buried with them.

Best Time to Visit: The best time to visit cemeteries in Ohio is during the spring.

Pass/Permit/Fees: It is free to visit the cemetery.

Closest City or Town: Akron

Physical Address: Mound Hill Cemetery, Seville, OH 44273

GPS Coordinates: 41.0108° N, 81.8535° W

Did You Know? Queen Victoria gave Anna Bates a diamond ring as a wedding gift.

The Glendale Steps

Ohio was one of the states hit hardest during the Great Depression. More than 25,000 people were out of work in Akron alone. The Worker's Progress Administration commissioned construction on the Glendale Steps in 1936 to get people back to work.

The Glendale Steps connect two neighborhoods in Akron to the public park that never was. The plans for the park were abandoned after a year, and the steps fell into disrepair until local citizens banded together to clean up and preserve them.

The 242 steps, which were laid by hand, lead down a 200-foot slope to a graveyard. A mural greets you halfway, and the area is decorated with flowers planted by Keep Akron Beautiful.

Best Time to Visit: The best time to visit is during the spring when all the flowers are in bloom.

Pass/Permit/Fees: It's free to climb the Glendale Steps.

Closest City or Town: Akron

Physical Address: 65-99 Glendale Ave, Akron, OH 44302

GPS Coordinates: 41.0858° N, 81.5232° W

Did You Know? During the cleanup, goats and alpacas were brought in as an eco-friendly alternative to gas mowers.

The Troll Hole Museum

The Troll Hole Museum is home to the largest collection of troll dolls in the world; owner-operator Sherry Groom won the Guinness World Records title in 2012. The museum features various themed rooms, including one for Princess Poppy, as well as a 10-foot-tall troll mountain and an obligatory troll bridge.

Sherry started her collection when she was just five years old and now shares over 3,000 dolls and 10,000 pieces of memorabilia in her museum.

The rarest trolls in the museum are a three-headed doll, ninja trolls, and a vintage Trollmobile.

Best Time to Visit: The museum is only open between December and April, and the best time to visit is on the weekends.

Pass/Permit/Fees: Entrance fees are $10 for adults, $8 for seniors, $6 for children under 12, and $3 for children ages 3 to 6.

Closest City or Town: Alliance

Physical Address: 228 E Main St, Alliance, OH 44601

GPS Coordinates: 40.9221° N, 81.1020° W

Did You Know? Fifteen trolls escaped the museum, and it's up to visitors to find them all before the tour ends.

Nelsonville Brick Park

In the mid-1800s, Nelsonville Brick was the biggest brick company in the state. By the 1880s, it was baking 25 million bricks per year in beehive-shaped kilns. Some of the kilns were later protected from demolition.

Nelsonville Brick Park features the protected ruins of these brick kilns, one of which is still fully intact. Visitors are encouraged to walk into and photograph the intact kiln; just remember to duck because the entryways are very low. There are also two huge smokestacks still standing.

The park is located right outside Nelsonville. It was built and dedicated on the original grounds of the Nelsonville Brick Company, which closed its doors in 1937.

Best Time to Visit: The best time to visit the park is in the spring.

Pass/Permit/Fees: It's free to visit the park.

Closest City or Town: Athens

Physical Address: 580 Lake Hope Dr, Nelsonville, OH 45764

GPS Coordinates: 39.5118° N, 82.2499° W

Did You Know? The grounds of the brick company were once paved with brick, and if you look closely, you might spot the remnants of the company's decorative star pavers.

Punderson Lake

When Lemuel Punderson, one of Ohio's earliest settlers, built his castled estate in the early 1800s, he had no idea how popular the area would become with future settlers, landowners, and tourists. During the summer, the sound of live music and the smells of barbeque fill the area. In the winter, the hills open for sledding, and the Mushers Trail opens for dogsledding.

After Labor Day, with smaller crowds, it is easier to explore Punderson State Park in winter. Snowmobiles are welcome at the lake, and there are three snowmobiling trails and two cross-country skiing trails.

During the summer months, these multi-use trails are open to hikers and bikers. Overnight options include full-hookup, electric, and non-electric sites, along with a selection of cabins. There are also 31 guest rooms available in the manor that was built on the site of Punderson's castle.

Best Time to Visit: The best time to visit the lake is during the winter between September and February.

Pass/Permit/Fees: Hiking, sledding, and visiting the lake are all free, and overnight stays start at $45 per night.

Closest City or Town: Bainbridge

Physical Address: 15192 Ravenna Rd, Burton, OH 44021

GPS Coordinates: 41.4534° N, 81.2058° W

Did You Know? Punderson is said to haunt the site.

Porter Creek Bridge Ruins

At the turn of the 20th century, the people of Ohio traveled on a network of trolley lines linking the northern cities of Cleveland and Toledo with Sandusky and Port Clinton. The Porter Creek Bridge was built in 1901 for trolleys headed to Huntington Beach. It remained in use until the Great Depression. All that remains of the bridge today are the giant bridge piers that tower above the trees.

Reaching the ruins is easy via the bike path that parallels Porter Creek Road. The path leads directly to the creek and under the ruins. Follow the path to a bridge, where you can cross the water and find more bridge pier ruins further into the woods.

Best Time to Visit: Spring is the best time to see the ruins.

Pass/Permit/Fees: It is free to visit the ruins.

Closest City or Town: Bay Village

Physical Address: You can park at or near the Lake Erie Nature & Science Center, 28728 Wolf Rd, Bay Village, OH 44140. Follow the bike path parallel to Porter Creek Rd.

GPS Coordinates: 41.4876° N, 81.9365° W

Did You Know? The last trolley car in Ohio took its final journey in 1954.

Bedford Reservation

Bedford Reservation was never logged, thanks in part to its rolling and rugged terrain, and visitors today can enjoy hikes, picnics, and camping in the seemingly never-ending forest. Over 20 hiking trails are equipped for mountain bikes and horseback riding.

The most popular hiking trails in Bedford are the Sagamore Creek Loop (3 miles) and Tinker's Creek Gorge Overlook Trail (5 miles). Sagamore Creek treats hikers to two waterfalls as it snakes through the forest, and Tinker's Creek Gorge provides views of Bridal Veil Falls and the gorge itself.

Visitors claim there are more than 70 waterfalls on the reservation. Off-trail exploration isn't recommended, but tours led by Cuyahoga Valley National Park take hikers off trail to some of the best-hidden falls.

Best Time to Visit: Visit during either March or April to see the falls at their fullest.

Pass/Permit/Fees: It's free to visit Bedford Reservation, and backpacking campsites start at $5 per day.

Closest City or Town: Bedford

Physical Address: 18753 Egbert Rd, Bedford, OH 44146

GPS Coordinates: 41.3786° N, 81.5428° W

Did You Know? The largest waterfall in the reservation is called the Great Falls of Tinker's Creek.

Dysart Woods

Dysart Woods is the last of the old oak forests in Ohio. Only 50 acres of the forest remain, and a laboratory established by Ohio University preserves the woods by preventing cutting and teaching future generations about this precious ecosystem.

Protection and preservation will not interfere with your exploration. Hike the Dysart Red and Blue loop trails to walk among the oaks. The trees are over 300 years old, and some are as much as 4 feet wide and 140 feet high.

The trails are likely to be overgrown because it is a forest lab, but hiking Dysart Woods is a unique natural experience that you won't find anywhere else in Ohio. Resist picking wildflowers during the spring, and don't bring in any food or drink. Picnic areas are available in nearby Barkcamp State Park.

Best Time to Visit: The best time to visit is from April through June.

Pass/Permit/Fees: It's free to visit and hike Dysart Woods.

Closest City or Town: Belmont

Physical Address: 61961 Dysart Woods Rd, Belmont, OH 43718

GPS Coordinates: 39.9821° N, 81.0009° W

Did You Know? The farmhouse at the entrance of the park was the original homestead of the Dysart family.

East Fork Lake

East Fork Lake is one of the busiest spots in the Cincinnati area during the summer. Visiting lakefront beaches, swimming, hiking, biking, and practicing at two archery ranges are just a few of the activities available. Backpackers can enjoy free campsites along the Steven Newman Worldwalker Perimeter Trail, which includes areas for horses.

The East Fork Long Loop trail (8 miles) does not have backpacking campsites but does lead hikers around the water and through the state park. Fern Hill Trail (1.4 miles), Whippoorwill Trail (0.5 miles), and the Williamsburg–Batavia Trail (6 miles) are all equipped for bikers. In the winter, the lake remains open for ice fishing and skating, and visitors are encouraged to go sledding and cross-country skiing.

Best Time to Visit: The best time to visit is between August and September.

Pass/Permit/Fees: It's free to visit East Fork Lake, and campsites start at $28 per night.

Closest City or Town: Bethel

Physical Address: East Fork State Park, 3294 Elklick Rd, Bethel, OH 45106

GPS Coordinates: 39.0226° N, 84.1502° W

Did You Know? There is access to the North Country National Scenic Trail here, one of the longest trails in the system linking Vermont to North Dakota.

William H. Harsha Lake

Built near two former gold mines, William H. Harsha Lake in East Fork State Park is a popular boating spot for locals. During the summer, the 40 miles of shoreline fill up with tourists and locals looking for some surf and sun. Five boat ramps make it easy to get onto the water, which is filled with bass, bluegill, crappie, and catfish.

Hiking and horseback-riding trails for all levels surround the lake, and select bridling trails lead directly to horse-ready campsites. The Beach Trail is a short and easy 1.3-mile hike that passes the shore, while the longer Twin Bridges trail (8.9 miles) loops around East Fork.

If you plan on visiting in the summer, expect a lot of creepy crawlies and spiderwebs. Overall, East Fork offers over 70 miles of trails to explore by foot, bike, or horse, and the water provides over 2,000 acres of boating, splashing, and swimming.

Best Time to Visit: The best time to hit the lake is in the summer.

Pass/Permit/Fees: Campsite prices will vary by season.

Closest City or Town: Bethel

Physical Address: East Fork State Park Beach, Park Rd 2, Bethel, OH 45106

GPS Coordinates: 39.0197° N, 84.1343° W

Did You Know? You can find sea fossils from 438 million years ago in and near the lake.

Big Muskie Bucket

Big Muskie was a giant bulldozer once used to mine the land where its memorial now sits. But "big" is an understatement. It is the largest bulldozer ever made. This giant piece of equipment weighed 13.5 tons and had to be assembled on-site in Ohio. It required 260 trucks and 340 train cars to ship. Today, all that's left is the bucket, which is roughly the size of a 12-car garage.

Climb inside Big Muskie Bucket and take a selfie before exploring the rest of Miner's Memorial Park, which is located in Jesse Owens State Park. There is a monument nearby honoring the employees of Central Ohio Coal Company, which commissioned Big Muskie in 1966.

Best Time to Visit: The best time to climb on the bucket is during late spring or early fall.

Pass/Permit/Fees: It is free to visit Jesse Owens State Park.

Closest City or Town: Caldwell

Physical Address: 4470 OH-78, McConnelsville, OH 43756

GPS Coordinates: 39.6995° N, 81.7313° W

Did You Know? Big Muskie moved more dirt than it took to carve out the Panama Canal.

Buzzard's Roost Nature Preserve

The terrain on the hiking trails in Buzzard's Roost is unique to Ohio, and the view of Paint Creek Gorge from the top of the South Point Lookout Trail (1.5 miles) is worth the climb. The trail parallels the gorge for most of the way, so be warned if you are afraid of heights.

Experienced hikers can reach an even better view via the Hoggard Trail (2.5 miles), which also passes an old pioneer homestead. The elevation gain is one of the quickest in the state; the highest point of the park rises 600 feet above the lowest, and poles and spikes are recommended.

If you've got the time and the season is right, take the spur trail to Blueberry Falls. The falls flow the best during the spring, but you may find more people on the trails during that time of year. Missing the hidden waterfalls sometimes means missing the crowds.

Best Time to Visit: The best time to visit is during the fall.

Pass/Permit/Fees: Campsites start at $25 per night.

Closest City or Town: Chillicothe

Physical Address: 514 Red Bird Ln, Chillicothe, OH 45601

GPS Coordinates: 39.32581° N, 83.0719° W

Did You Know? Don't forget to look up to spot vultures and buzzards circling above—various species nest in the area.

American Sign Museum

Take a tour of the American Sign Museum to get a unique perspective of American history. Over 3,000 neon signs, movie posters, highway markers, and more tell the story of American culture, commerce, and technology. Owner Tod Swormstedt has been involved with signs all his life. His father edited and eventually owned the sign industry's trade journal, and Tod was inspired to open the museum in 1999. It was expanded and moved to its current location to accommodate some of the collection's largest signs. Mr. Swormstedt hosts guided tours. Highlights include a McDonald's sign with a single arch and an original Big Boy statue with the slingshot in his pocket.

Best Time to Visit: Visit the museum on Sundays to get a free guided tour with your ticket.

Pass/Permit/Fees: Adults cost $15. Children, seniors, military personnel, and first responders cost $10.

Closest City or Town: Cincinnati

Physical Address: 1330 Monmouth Ave, Cincinnati, OH 45225

GPS Coordinates: 39.1435° N, 84.5401° W

Did You Know? Neonworks of Cincinnati shows visitors how they restore neon signs inside the museum.

Cincinnati Observatory

This is the oldest professional observatory in the country. It operates as a 19th-century observatory and houses 11-inch and 16-inch telescopes. The 11-inch Merz and Mahler telescope, built in 1845, is believed to be the oldest in operation in the world.

The observatory is located in the heart of a historic residential neighborhood. If you visit during the day, walk a block to East Hyde Park for a picnic or explore the local restaurants and coffee shops nearby.

Best Time to Visit: For day tours, visit during the week between 11 a.m. and 2 p.m. For night tours and stargazing, visit on Saturday nights.

Pass/Permit/Fees: It costs $10 for adults and $5 for children to tour the observatory. Event prices vary.

Closest City or Town: Cincinnati

Physical Address: 3489 Observatory Pl, Cincinnati, OH 45208

GPS Coordinates: 39.1392° N, 84.4226° W

Did You Know? President John Quincy Adams gave his last public speech at the observatory's cornerstone ceremony.

Cincinnati Subway

The state of Ohio has attempted every type of rail travel imaginable, from trains and trolleys to the ill-fated Cincinnati subway. The original plan was to drain the canals and build the rapid rail system in its place, but hefty price tags and the cost of WWI slowed the project before the Great Depression finally snuffed it out for good.

Miles of tunnels and the four original stations built in 1920 remain underground, and tours were given to the public until they were deemed unsafe by the City of Cincinnati.

Today, visitors can explore the abandoned tunnels at their own risk. Most entrances are gated or sealed off, but urban explorers can still get inside if they know where to look.

Best Time to Visit: The best time to visit is during the fall.

Pass/Permit/Fees: It costs nothing to visit the Cincinnati subway.

Closest City or Town: Cincinnati

Physical Address: From downtown Cincinnati, merge onto I-75 N and take Exit 3 for Hopple Street. Turn right on Hopple, then right onto Martin Luther King. You can see the entrance to the subway over the concrete fence.

GPS Coordinates: 39.1366° N, 84.5328° W

Did You Know? The original price tag for the subway was $6 million in 1920, the equivalent of $13.6 million today.

Cincinnati Yellow Lamps

Cincinnati's streetlamps are unlike those in any other city. The Yellow Lamps mark areas where there are raised medians in the road, which some locals argue were once streetcar platforms. There is no proof either way, but the lamps are distinct enough to attract the attention of curious tourists who haven't seen anything like them.

The Yellow Lamps are known for their domed yellow globes, which earned them the affectionate nickname of "Turtle Lights" and their whimsical aluminum canopies. There are 50 Yellow Lamps still left in the city; the GPS coordinates here will lead you to the one on Plum Street.

Best Time to Visit: Visit at night after the sun sets to see the lamps light up with their signature yellow glow.

Pass/Permit/Fees: The lamps are dotted all around the city for every driver and pedestrian to see for free.

Closest City or Town: Cincinnati

Physical Address: The funny little lamp is located at the intersection of Central Pkwy and Plum St, Cincinnati, OH 45202.

GPS Coordinates: 39.1065° N, 84.5193° W

Did You Know? The city says it will not replace any more fallen or damaged Yellow Lights, but the latest fallen lamp was replaced within a few weeks in August of 2014.

Loveland Castle

This isn't a medieval castle, but it sure looks like one. Loveland Castle, also known as Chateau Laroche, was built by Harry Andrews at the age of 55. He made the bricks from milk cartons and cement and added 110,000 buckets of dirt and stone.

Andrews himself flattened the land surrounding the castle to build the road to the entrance, the moat around the castle, and the garden and orchard. The museum within the castle includes a full set of armor, the Andrews family coat-of-arms, and a re-creation of a medieval tower prison.

Best time to Visit: The best time to tour the castle is weekends in November and December.

Passes/Permits/Fees: It's $5 per person to tour the castle, and children under 5 are free.

Closest City or Town: Cincinnati

Physical Address: 12075 Shore Dr, Loveland, OH 45140

GPS Coordinates: 39.2849° N, 84.2656° W

Did You Know? The coat-of-arms on display was granted to the Andrews family in 1534 by King Henry VIII.

Lucky Cat Museum

The Lucky Cat, or Maneki-Neko as it is known in Japan, is believed to bring monetary fortune and good luck to its owner. When its little paw waves, people are drawn to it and, hopefully, into your business. Over 2,000 of them will beckon you into the Lucky Cat Museum.

The Lucky Cat Museum collects and displays all versions of the Lucky Cat figurine, including traditional Japanese cats, modern cats created by Japanese and American artists, ceramic cats, plush cats, and even household items and stationery featuring the lucky feline. The cats displayed belong to a personal collection, and the owner opens the museum for visitors by appointment.

Best Time to Visit: Appointments to see the museum are available between Monday and Thursday from 3 to 6 p.m.

Pass/Permit/Fees: It's free to visit the museum, but donations are welcome.

Closest City or Town: Cincinnati

Physical Address: 2511 Essex Pl, Cincinnati, OH 45206

GPS Coordinates: 39.1274° N, 84.4992° W

Did You Know? It's a long-standing Japanese belief that when a cat is washing its face, a visitor will come, which is why the Lucky Cat statues look like they are waving.

Pyramid Hill Sculpture Park

This park is where nature and monumental art collide. There are over 65 sculptures across 335 acres of green grass and gardens to explore. Visitors can rent "art carts" to zip around from sculpture to sculpture.

This is your chance to experience art, history, and nature all at once. Miles of hiking trails lead visitors to various sculptures and creations, and information about local wildlife in the park is scattered throughout. There is even a 19th-century pioneer house on site. The park is open all year long.

Best Time to Visit: Visit on Sundays or Mondays when the Ancient Sculpture Museum is open too.

Pass/Permit/Fees: It costs $8 per adult and $3 per child to explore the outdoor museum.

Closest City or Town: Cincinnati

Physical Address: 1763 Hamilton Cleves Rd, Hamilton, OH 45013

GPS Coordinates: 39.3654° N, 84.5777° W

Did You Know? Park creator Harry T. Wilks didn't trust private landowners and turned the park into a nonprofit to protect the land and the art.

Rookwood Ice Cream Parlor

In Cincinnati's old Union Terminal sits an ice cream parlor frozen in time. Originally a tea room, the parlor was a staple in a terminal that also featured a barbershop and restaurants. Today, the terminal is a museum, and Rookwood Ice Cream Parlor serves a local favorite: Graeter's.

The parlor is called Rookwood for the famous tile used in its design. Rookwood, started by local Maria Longworth Nichols Store, was a Cincinnati ceramic company that dominated the state of Ohio and most of the east coast.

Best Time to Visit: Visit in October or November to avoid the crowds of tourists.

Pass/Permit/Fees: The entrance fee for adults and teens ages 13 and up is $16.50. Seniors and children under 12 are $12.50, and younger children are $7.50. The cost of ice cream will vary.

Closest City or Town: Cincinnati

Physical Address: 1301 Western Ave, Cincinnati, OH 45203

GPS Coordinates: 39.1104° N, 84.5373° W

Did You Know? Rookwood tiles are also used throughout the New York subway system.

The Dexter Mausoleum

The Dexter Mausoleum in Spring Grove Cemetery is the final resting place for the Dexter family of whiskey barons. The mausoleum is designed to look like a Gothic funeral monument. It is located in Section 20 of the graveyard.

Only family members are allowed inside, but visitors can photograph the exterior. Visitors may also note a peculiar marker for Charles Dexter. Due to family drama surrounding the estate, after Charles Dexter died without a male heir, young Carroll Dexter Walker had to change her name to receive her $20,000 inheritance.

Best Time to Visit: The best time to visit the cemetery is in the spring.

Pass/Permit/Fees: It's free to visit Spring Grove Cemetery.

Closest City or Town: Cincinnati

Physical Address: 4521 Spring Grove Ave, Cincinnati, OH 45232

GPS Coordinates: 39.1745° N, 84.5250° W

Did You Know? The buttresses on the mausoleum are the only two symmetrical ones of their kind in Cincinnati.

The Mushroom House

Artist Terry Brown wanted to create a home better related to more natural dimensions than most homes. What seems like madness is actually the result of meticulous geometry.

The wooden shingles are cut by hand to look like the underside of a mushroom, and the domed addition to the home looks like fungi. The glass sunroom on top of the domed roof completes the magical structure and is decorated with beautiful stained-glass fixtures.

The home is still a private residence, but visitors are welcome to photograph the Mushroom House from the street.

Best Time to Visit: The best time to see the Mushroom House is early afternoons in the fall.

Pass/Permit/Fees: It's free to stop, see, and photograph the home.

Closest City or Town: Cincinnati

Physical Address: 3331 Erie Ave, Cincinnati, OH 45208

GPS Coordinates: 39.1411° N, 84.4237° W

Did You Know? In some areas of the home, the wooden shingles are as much as 10 inches thick.

A Christmas Story House and Museum

Step into one of the most iconic movies of the holiday season. The exterior remains just as it was when the neighbors gathered around to see the "major award" in the window, and the interior is decorated for Christmas.

A Christmas Story House is a moment frozen in time, and the museum across the street showcases the props, behind-the-scenes photos, and facts about the film that even diehard fans might not know. The Bumpus House next door is available for overnight stays.

Best Time to Visit: Winter is the busiest season, so visit earlier in the fall.

Pass/Permit/Fees: General admission is $15. Seniors are $14, and children are $11. Overnight stays are available, starting at $195 per night.

Closest City or Town: Cleveland

Physical Address: 3159 W 11th St, Cleveland, OH 44109

GPS Coordinates: 41.4687° N, 81.6874° W

Did You Know? Only the exterior of the home was used in the movies.

Balto the Sled Dog at the Cleveland Museum of Natural History

Balto was a sled dog from Nome, Alaska—so, what is he doing in Cleveland? You can thank George Kimble, an early 20th-century businessman. After delivering diphtheria medicine across the 167-mile Iditarod Trail in just six days, Balto and the sled dog team were rewarded by being sold to a dime museum in Los Angeles.

When George learned of this, he immediately raised money to have Balto and the team shipped to live more comfortably in the Cleveland Zoo in 1925. Balto is now on display in the Museum of Natural History.

Best Time to Visit: Weekday mornings are the best time to visit, but the museum is closed on Mondays.

Pass/Permit/Fees: Adults are $17, and children ages 3 through 18 are $15. Seniors and college students can get in for $14 with ID.

Closest City or Town: Cleveland

Physical Address: 1 Wade Oval Dr, Cleveland, OH 44106

GPS Coordinates: 41.5117° N, 81.6129° W

Did You Know? Balto and the six-dog team were welcomed to Cleveland with a parade in Public Square.

Buckland Museum of Witchcraft and Magick

Raymond Buckland's hobby for folklore and the supernatural became one of the first anthropological museums of paganism in the United States. The Buckland Museum of Witchcraft and Magick displays more than 500 artifacts from around the world, including historical items from the Salem Witch Trials.

Pass/Permit/Fees: Visiting the museum requires a ticket, and guests are encouraged to buy tickets online to choose their entry times.

Best Time to Visit: This museum is open year-round.

Pass/Permit/Fees: Adult admission is $7. Seniors cost $6, and children cost $5.

Closest City or Town: Cleveland

Physical Address: 2155 Broadview Rd, Cleveland, OH 44109

GPS Coordinates: 41.4382° N, 81.6998° W

Did You Know? The Metropolitan Museum of Art featured some of Buckland's artifacts in a special exhibit.

Chagrin Falls

Try a little time travel on your vacation for a trip to Chagrin Falls. The vintage Ohio village was established in the early 19th century around the series of cascading waterfalls that tumble through the heart of downtown.

The best view of the waterfalls is from between Main Street and Bell Street, situated conveniently by some of the village's most popular snack stops. Follow the wooden steps from the street down to the bottom of the falls for an even better view.

The village of Chagrin Falls has preserved its turn-of-the-century storefronts while transforming them into niche boutiques, savory restaurants, and many other modern interpretations of local fare. You don't want to miss a trip to the Chagrin Historical Society, and you have to try an ice cream cone from the locally owned Popcorn Shop.

Best Time to Visit: The best time to see the falls is in April.

Pass/Permit/Fees: It's free to visit the falls.

Closest City or Town: Chagrin Falls

Physical Address: N Main St, Chagrin Falls, OH 44022

GPS Coordinates: 41.4313° N, 81.39214° W

Did You Know? Chagrin Falls High School is one of the top high schools in the country.

Cleveland Trust Rotunda Building

Built in 1907, the Rotunda Building was the downtown branch of the Cleveland Trust Company, one of the first banking institutions in the city.

The rotunda fits neatly on the corner of Euclid and 9th Avenues. It was designed by George B. Post, the architect who also designed the New York Stock Exchange, and its 85-foot-high rotunda features a stained-glass dome.

This historic financial landmark stood empty for nearly two decades before it was salvaged by Cuyahoga County and Heinen's, a local grocery chain that turned the Rotunda Building into its first downtown location in 2015. Feel free to pick up a snack while you're there.

Best Time to Visit: Weekdays are the best time to visit.

Pass/Permit/Fees: It's free to visit the Rotunda Building.

Closest City or Town: Cleveland

Physical Address: 900 Euclid Ave, Cleveland, OH 44115

GPS Coordinates: 41.5003° N, 81.6862° W

Did You Know? The murals inside were painted by Francis Davis Millet, who later lost his life on the *Titanic*.

Cuyahoga Jack-Knife Bridge #464

This bridge is a relic from a time when steam and steel dominated Cleveland. Miles of train track once linked the city and carried shipments of coal, iron, and more. The Cuyahoga Jack-Knife Bridge is a 19th-century drawbridge that made a way for trains to cross the Cuyahoga River while still letting boats and freighters pass through. It stands at 334 feet tall and stretches 201 feet in length across the river.

Visitors can park near the bridge or along nearby streets. You cannot miss it from Main Avenue because the red metal reaches toward the sky despite being covered with grapevines. You're allowed to walk the track bed but refrain from climbing on the structure.

Best Time to Visit: The best time to visit is on weekdays when most street parking is free.

Pass/Permit/Fees: It's free to visit the bridge.

Closest City or Town: Cleveland

Physical Address: Parking, 1148 Main Ave, Cleveland, OH 44113

GPS Coordinates: 41.9182° N, 81.7070° W

Did You Know? If you visit during the summer, you might spy a wedding party taking photos by the bridge.

36

Dittrick Medical Museum

Originally a part of the Cleveland Medical Library Association, the Dittrick Medical Museum began as a tool for doctors to document their work and professional experiences. It has since evolved into one of the most extensive collections of medical instruments and historical artifacts in the country.

Exhibits also highlight letters from Charles Darwin, the advancement of contraception and childbirth, and reproductions of 19th- and 20th-century doctor's offices. The Blaufox Hall of Diagnostic Instruments houses a century's worth of medical instruments.

Best Time to Visit: Visit the museum during the fall when it's less likely to be crowded.

Pass/Permit/Fees: Visitors pay $11 to enter the museum.

Closest City or Town: Cleveland

Physical Address: The Allen Memorial Medical Library, 11000 Euclid Ave, Cleveland, OH 44106

GPS Coordinates: 41.5059° N, 81.6085° W

Did You Know? The museum serves as a study center for university students as well as a museum for the public.

Edgewater Beach

The 2,400 feet of Edgewater Beach, the surrounding 6,000 feet of shoreline, and Lakefront Reservation recently underwent a makeover. Now, locals and tourists can enjoy a new definition of lakeside living in Ohio. Visitors are encouraged to bring their bikes and dogs to hit the multipurpose trail that leads from the beach through downtown and back again. But you don't have to venture that far for a good time. Stay on the beach and take in the view of downtown Cleveland from the shore, or pack a late-night snack for a sunset picnic.

Edgewater Beach is open for swimmers, waders, parasailers, kayakers, and anglers looking to try their luck off Edgewater Fishing Pier. Pick up your supplies from the Pier Grille and Bait Shop, and hit the pier or the rock jetty to launch your own canoe.

Best Time to Visit: To get the most out of your trip to the beach, visit during the summer.

Pass/Permit/Fees: It's free to visit the beach, and cabana rentals are available.

Closest City or Town: Cleveland

Physical Address: 7600 Cleveland Memorial Shoreway, Cleveland OH 44102

GPS Coordinates: 41.49038° N, 81.73781°

Did You Know? Water quality at Edgewater Beach is monitored daily by the Northeast Ohio Regional Sewer District.

Helltown

Are you brave enough to explore a ghost town riddled with rumors of human sacrifice and satanic rituals? Then take a hike to the deserted township of Boston, Ohio, in Cuyahoga Valley National Park. Boston Township is more commonly known as Helltown for the creepy legends and myths surrounding the abandoned rural village. However, the townspeople were not scared off by giant mutant pythons.

The farmers left the town in 1974 when the land was designated a national park by President Ford. Hikers and bikers can explore the town's cemetery and slaughterhouse and an abandoned school bus. As you tour the ghost town, appreciate those who sacrificed to preserve the forests.

Best Time to Visit: The best time to visit is in the fall.

Pass/Permit/Fees: It's free to visit the national park.

Closest City or Town: Cleveland

Physical Address: Boston Trailhead, 1498 Boston Mills Rd West, Peninsula, OH 44264

GPS Coordinates: 41.2633° N, 81.5572° W

Did You Know? An illegal toxic dumpsite at nearby Krejci Dump feeds rumors of the giant Peninsula Python living in the woods.

Hillandale Bridge

Hillandale Bridge is truly a bridge to nowhere. The nearly century-old bridge never stood a chance of reaching completion after the 1929 market crash. Originally designed with an expensive, elaborate S-curve to connect the two valleys, it now sits unfinished in the middle of Hillandale Park. Remnants of street lamps line the road on your way to the bridge, but nature is slowly reclaiming the structure, covering the arches and beams with ivy.

To reach the bridge, follow the old brick road in Hillandale Park. Visitors are allowed to walk on the bridge, but be careful because of the crumbling construction.

Best Time to Visit: Walk the bridge during the fall to appreciate the changing of the leaves.

Pass/Permit/Fees: It's free to explore Hillandale Park and the bridge.

Closest City or Town: Cleveland

Physical Address: 27560 Tremaine Dr, Euclid, OH 44132

GPS Coordinates: 41.5915° N, 81.4908° W

Did You Know? No car has ever driven on the bridge.

Franklin Castle

Hannes Tiedemann, the original owner and builder of Franklin Castle, experienced more death and tragedy than any man should in a single lifetime, leaving behind a legacy that haunts the property to this day. Tiedemann's 15-year-old daughter was the first to die in the home in 1881, followed by his elderly mother. Later, Tiedemann buried his wife and four more children who died in infancy. Many believe the family still lingers in the home, especially when doors open and close without warning and ghostly footsteps echo in the hall.

Franklin Castle is private property, and tours are not available. However, visitors can photograph the exterior of the home.

Best Time to Visit: The best time to visit is in April or May.

Pass/Permit/Fees: It is free to see the exterior of the home.

Closest City or Town: Cleveland

Physical Address: 4308 Franklin Blvd, Cleveland, OH 44113

GPS Coordinates: 41.4858° N, 81.7165° W

Did You Know? Franklin Castle was once owned by Judy Garland's last husband, actor Mickey Deans.

Frozen Cleveland Lighthouse

The West Pierhead Lighthouse on Lake Erie is more commonly known as the Frozen Lighthouse. Every winter, it is encased in layers of ice crystals. It started in 2010, when gale-force winds churned up water, crossed the lighthouse's break wall, and repeatedly splashed onto the structure.

Now, the layers get thicker each year, transforming the lighthouse into more of an icy castle. The best way to view the Frozen Lighthouse is from Wendy Park in downtown Cleveland, or hop on a boat for a closer look.

Best Time to Visit: Visit in January or February to see the Pierhead Lighthouse in all its icy glory.

Pass/Permit/Fees: It is free to visit Wendy Park and see the lighthouse.

Closest City or Town: Cleveland

Physical Address: 2800 Whiskey Island Dr, Cleveland, OH 44102

GPS Coordinates: 41.5092° N, 81.7177° W

Did You Know? The wind, water, and ice have caused the lighthouse to lean to the right.

James A. Garfield's Memorial and Tomb

President James A. Garfield, who served only 200 days in office, is interred in one of the most elaborate memorials in the country. It is also the only memorial to have a former president's casket on public display. Ohioans raised $135,000 to build the 180-foot-high tomb; it features stained-glass windows, a 12-foot statue of President Garfield, and views of Lake Erie from the balcony. Five bas-relief panels tell the story of the president's life. Garfield's wife Lucretia, his daughter Mary, and Mary's husband, John Stanley Brown, are also buried in the tomb.

Best Time to Visit: The best time to visit is between June and October, when the memorial is open to the public.

Passes/Permits/Fees: It's free to visit the memorial.

Closest City or Town: Cleveland

Physical Address: 12316 Euclid Ave, Cleveland, OH 44106

GPS Coordinates: 41.5101° N, 81.5912° W

Did You Know? Robert Todd Lincoln, son of Abraham Lincoln, was there when Garfield was shot.

Jesse Owens Statue

Jesse Owens's family moved to town when he was nine, and he earned a name for himself and his city. Ironically, Jesse Owens's given name is James Cleveland. It didn't surprise anyone who knew Owens at Ohio State when he won four gold medals in Berlin, but he wasn't given the hero's homecoming he deserved due to state segregation laws.

President Eisenhower recognized him in 1955 as an ambassador, and in 1979, he earned the first Presidential Medal of Freedom. The 8-foot-tall statue in Fort Huntington Park, erected in 1982, depicts Owens as larger than life.

Best Time to Visit: The best time to visit is in August on the anniversary of Owens's epic wins in Berlin.

Pass/Permit/Fees: It is free to visit Huntington Park and see the statue.

Closest City or Town: Cleveland

Physical Address: 299-1 W Lakeside Ave, Cleveland, OH 44113

GPS Coordinates: 41.5025° N, 81.6982° W

Did You Know? Owens introduced himself at his new school in Cleveland as "J.C.," which became "Jesse."

Land of Warres

Artist and self-proclaimed Geographer-at-Large Eames Demetrios created Kcymaerxthaere, a fictional universe that is much like a storybook, where every page is a different location. One of these pages overlaps with our world in Cleveland.

The Land of Warres is marked by a plaque on a brick wall on Perkins Street in midtown, connecting the Warren (organisms without metabolism) with other creatures in Kcymaerxthaere's story.

For the human explorers in this universe, the Land of Warres is surrounded by abandoned buildings and warehouses that make for unique photo-ops.

Best Time to Visit: The best time to explore Kcymaerxthaere in Cleveland is in April or September, when the weather is mild.

Pass/Permit/Fees: It is free to visit Warren sites.

Closest City or Town: Cleveland

Physical Address: 4701 Perkins Ave, Cleveland, OH 44103

GPS Coordinates: 41.5069° N, 81.6547° W

Did You Know? Kcymaerxthaere touches our universe in 90 spots across 18 different countries.

Sidaway Bridge

The ruins of Sidaway Bridge stand as a stark reminder of Ohio's deeply segregated past. The suspension bridge was built in 1939 to replace the previous pedestrian bridge and make room for trains to cross. It linked the Kinsman and Jackowo neighborhoods.

Jackowo was predominantly Polish, but by the mid-1900s, the neighborhood of Kinsman was predominantly Black. Young Black children from Kinsman would cross Sidaway Bridge on their way to school in Jackowo until riots broke out in 1966 and white citizens attempted to dismantle the bridge and set it on fire.

The bridge has been closed ever since, and the entrances on either side remain blocked off by overgrowth and *No Trespassing* signs.

Best Time to Visit: The best time to visit is in the winter when the bridge ices over and is covered in snow.

Pass/Permit/Fees: It's free to see the bridge.

Closest City or Town: Cleveland

Physical Address: The bridge is a short walk from the corner of Anita Kennedy Ave, Cleveland, OH 44104

GPS Coordinates: 41.4802° N, 81.6428° W

Did You Know? The attempted arson on the bridge was later used in the court case that desegregated Ohio schools.

Squaw Rock

In 1885, artist and blacksmith Henry Church set out to capture the Native American experience at the hands of white settlers. He created an intricate sandstone carving of a quiver of arrows in the four phases of the moon, a Native American woman in a shell, and a baby in a papoose.

Other carvings along Squaw Rock include a giant serpent, an eagle, a frontiersman, and the earliest capital buildings in Washington D.C. Squaw Rock is located in South Chagrin Reservation and can be reached via the Squaw Rock Trail. The trail is a little over a half-mile long but is very strenuous through uneven land and rock.

Best Time to Visit: The best time to visit is in winter when the surrounding waterfalls are frozen like sculptures.

Pass/Permit/Fees: It's free to see Squaw Rock.

Closest City or Town: Cleveland

Physical Address: Henry Church Rock Parking, Bridle Trail and Loops, Bentleyville, OH 44022

GPS Coordinates: 41.4169° N, 81.41518° W

Did You Know? It is said that Church carved his creations by lantern light.

Steamship William G. Mather

The SS *William G. Mather* was one of the fastest freighters on the Great Lakes. During WWII, President Roosevelt ordered the Mather to lead a 13-freighter convoy through a frozen Lake Erie to Duluth, Minnesota. The *William G. Mather* was the first steamship equipped with radar and a fully automated boiler system, and it was the last of the Cleveland-Cliffs Iron Company's ships to be decommissioned. It now operates as a floating maritime museum and is part of the Great Lakes Science Center. Climb aboard the steamship, where you can step into the engine room, cargo holds, and sleeping quarters before walking the 618-foot-long deck.

Best Time to Visit: The best time to visit is in September or October when the weather is nice, and the tourists are gone.

Pass/Permit/Fees: Entrance fees are $9 per adult, $7 per senior, and $6 per child 12 and under.

Closest City or Town: Cleveland

Physical Address: 601 Erieside Ave, Cleveland, OH 44114

GPS Coordinates: 41.5089° N, 81.6977° W

Did You Know? One of the ship's captains, Harry Anderson, was among the first group of volunteers who restored the vessel in 1987.

St. Theodosius Cathedral

The St. Theodosius Cathedral is one of the finest examples of Russian architecture in the United States. It was erected in 1913 through its parishioners' donations and has been an iconic piece of the Cleveland skyline for over a century.

During the Russian Revolution and subsequent Russian Civil War, immigrants came to Cleveland and joined the St. Theodosius parish. The church features 13 onion-shaped domes representing Jesus and the 12 apostles, and it contains many icons imported from Russia.

Best Time to Visit: The best time to visit is during Christmas when the choir performs the Annual Cleveland Landmark Christmas Concert.

Pass/Permit/Fees: It's free to visit the cathedral.

Closest City or Town: Cleveland

Physical Address: 733 Starkweather Ave, Cleveland, OH 44113

GPS Coordinates: 41.4775° N, 81.6817° W

Did You Know? The cathedral cost $70,000 (over $1.9 million today) and is believed to have been partially funded by Czar Nikolas II.

The Cleveland Arcade

Built in 1890, these two 9-story buildings feature art galleries, tea shops, spas, restaurants, a hotel, and a post office. The buildings are connected by a 5-story arcade that domes into a glass skylight spanning 300 feet across the shopping center. The Cleveland Arcade is recognized as one of the first indoor shopping malls in America. It was also the first building in Cleveland to be listed on the National Register of Historic Places.

The Cleveland Arcade is the oldest but not the only one in Cleveland. The nearby 5th Street Arcades feature a food court, Marriott hotel, and more shopping.

Best Time to Visit: The best time to visit the arcade is between October and February.

Pass/Permit/Fees: It's free to walk the arcade, but vendor prices will vary.

Closest City or Town: Cleveland

Physical Address: 401 Euclid Ave, Cleveland, OH 44115

GPS Coordinates: 41.5001° N, 81.6903° W

Did You Know? The arcade cost $875,000 to construct (the equivalent of $26.25 million today), and John D. Rockefeller was one of the original financiers.

The Haserot Angel

The official name of the *Haserot Angel* sculpture in Cleveland's Lakeview Cemetery is "The Angel of Death Victorious." She weeps black tears over the Haserot family, famous in Cleveland for starting a successful canned-goods business.

The black tears have earned her the title of Weeping Angel. It's naturally caused by the erosion of the bronze sculpture, but it still creates an eerie ambiance in one of the most famous cemeteries in Ohio. The cemetery has over 100,000 graves, most of whom belong to famous Ohioans, including presidents, bank robbers, and business moguls.

Best Time to Visit: The best time to visit is between October and January, when the statute looks its creepiest.

Pass/Permit/Fees: It's free to visit Lakeview Cemetery.

Closest City or Town: Cleveland

Physical Address: 12316 Euclid Ave, Cleveland, OH 44106

GPS Coordinates: 41.5132° N, 81.5904° W

Did You Know? Herman Matzen, the sculptor of the *Haserot Angel*, is also buried in Lakeview Cemetery.

Warner and Swasey Observatory

The Warner and Swasey Observatory was home to key astronomical discoveries, including the spiral shape of the Milky Way galaxy and the red giants (colder stars) at the heart of it. But this scientific landmark was put out of commission in the 1950s by the light pollution from ever-expanding Cleveland.

The observatory's 24-inch telescope was moved to the Kitt Peak National Observatory in Arizona, leaving behind the domes that once housed two of the strongest telescopes of their time. Visitors can only photograph the exterior; the interior is private property.

Best Time to Visit: This is accessible anytime.

Pass/Permit/Fees: It's free to see the observatory.

Closest City or Town: Cleveland

Physical Address: 1975 N Taylor Rd, Cleveland, OH 44112

GPS Coordinates: 41.5363° N, 81.5685° W

Did You Know? The property's owner, Nayyir Al Mahdi, had planned to turn the observatory into a museum until he was arrested for fraud in 2007.

West Side Market

West Side Market is the oldest open-air market in Cleveland, but the original market operated just across the street from its current location. Cleveland grew too fast for the original, and the market underwent two major remodels before settling on its current spot in 1912.

The concourse inside has stalls for up to 100 vendors, and the outdoor produce market provides space for 85 stalls. Most of the vendors here belong to the original families who set up shop in 1912, and many feature delicacies from Ireland, Germany, Russia, Poland, and Greece.

Stroll through the market to find something to munch. You'll find any kind of snack you can think of, including fresh meats, fruit, veggies, and baked goods.

Best Time to Visit: Wednesday mornings are the best time to tour the market.

Pass/Permit/Fees: It's free to enter the market, but vendor prices will vary.

Closest City or Town: Cleveland

Physical Address: 1979 W 25th St, Cleveland, OH 44113

GPS Coordinates: 41.4848° N, 81.7031° W

Did You Know? The market did not open on Sundays until 2016.

Worden's Ledges

The sandstone cliffs seem out of place in the middle of the woods, but their smooth surfaces make for excellent carvings, as Noble Stuart discovered. Stuart, the husband of Nettie Worden, carved multiple figures into the rock during the 1940s. The carvings speak to his youth and the people he knew. As you hike the trail, you may recognize George Washington, Ty Cobb, Thomas Jefferson, and perhaps others. There is even a carving of Stuart's father-in-law, Hiram Worden, the original owner of the property.

The trail to Worden's Ledges is a 0.7-mile loop that is relatively easy and fit for horseback riding. Keep your eyes peeled for wildlife as you explore because deer are often spotted in the area.

Best Time to Visit: The best time to hike to Worden's Ledges is between April and October.

Pass/Permit/Fees: It's free to hike the Worden's Ledges Loop Trail.

Closest City or Town: Cleveland

Physical Address: Wordens Ledges Loop Trail, Hinckley, OH 44233

GPS Coordinates: 41.2038° N, 81.7188° W

Did You Know? Locals originally thought Hiram Worden's son Frank created the carvings.

Yorkie Doodle Dandy Memorial

Smokey is the smallest war hero ever, clocking in at barely 4 pounds, but she earned herself the name "Yorkie Doodle Dandy" during WWII for various heroic acts. She warned American soldiers of snipers and incoming artillery, boosted morale in military hospitals with her repertoire of tricks, and even managed to carry a radio line through a pipe after the telegraph joints collapsed.

She survived 150 air raids and a typhoon. After the war, Smokey was awarded her own television show and visited veterans' hospitals throughout the country. She remained with William Wynne, the soldier who kept her throughout the war, until the day she died in 1956.

Best Time to Visit: The best time to visit Smokey is in the spring.

Pass/Permit/Fees: It's free to visit the memorial.

Closest City or Town: Cleveland

Physical Address: Valley Pkwy, Lakewood, OH 44107

GPS Coordinates: 41.4668° N, 81.8333° W

Did You Know? Smokey was the first-ever recorded therapy dog.

Clifton Gorge Falls

Clifton Gorge Falls are in the heart of the Clifton Gorge Nature Preserve. The water races through a gorge carved millions of years ago by a massive glacier that sliced through Campbell Hill during the Ice Age.

You'll catch sight of rapids, swells, and a pristine blue pond on your way to the waterfall. Clifton Gorge is a man-made waterfall that once powered the Clifton Mill. The mill's wheel remains, along with a covered bridge and other turn-of-the-century buildings.

If you follow the Narrows Trail, which starts just past the old mill, you will catch sight of more tiny waterfalls through the trees. The trail ends at Amphitheatre Falls, where a tiny stream plummets 25 feet into the gorge. Take advantage of the observation decks along the boardwalk for even better views.

Best Time to Visit: The best time to see the falls is in the spring.

Pass/Permit/Fees: It's free to visit the falls.

Closest City or Town: Clifton

Physical Address: 2381 OH-343, Yellow Springs, OH 45387

GPS Coordinates: 39.7942° N, 83.8315° W

Did You Know? Daniel Boone famously explored this area in the 1700s.

Arnold Schwarzenegger Statue

The statue honoring this pop culture icon and politician is located right outside the convention center where Arnold won the Mr. World competition in 1970. The statue stands at 8 feet tall and weighs over 600 pounds, so take the time to bask in the glory of sinewy muscle and chiseled features.

History was in the making that day in 1970 when Arnold befriended Jim Lorimer, the event's coordinator. The two worked together, eventually creating the Arnold Classic, a fitness competition that has taken place every year in Columbus since 1989.

You can easily spot the statue from the street, and parking is available on the streets around the convention center.

Best Time to Visit: The best time to see the statue is during the spring when the weather is warmer.

Pass/Permit/Fees: It's free to stop by and see the statue.

Closest City or Town: Columbus

Physical Address: 486 N High St #474, Columbus, OH 43215

GPS Coordinates: 39.9723° N, 83.0023° W

Did You Know? A meme of Arnold sleeping next to his statue in a sleeping bag went viral in 2015.

As We Are: The Ultimate Selfie Machine

If a picture is worth a thousand words, what will your selfie say when it's projected in 3D at 14 feet? Located in the atrium of the Greater Columbus Convention Center, the Ultimate Selfie Machine will take 32 pictures of you and then project your face onto the "big head," a screen made of 850,000 LED lights that are designed to look like a human head. Your photo will display for 30 seconds before looping through others' selfies. The big head was created from 3D scans of 5,000 different people, and your selfie may be stretched or squashed to fit. It's deliberate and forces us all to question the relationship between how we see ourselves and how we are seen by others.

Best Time to Visit: This is a popular destination, so visit during the offseason in late fall to miss the crowds.

Pass/Permit/Fees: It's free to take your photo, and visitors can take up to three selfies.

Closest City or Town: Columbus

Physical Address: Greater Columbus Convention Center, 400 N High St, Columbus, OH 43215

GPS Coordinates: 39.9734° N, 83.0020° W

Did You Know? As We Are defaults to diversity, and uncommon skin tones and features are displayed more frequently.

Athens Lunatic Asylum

If you're visiting Ohio in the fall, one of the most haunted spots in the state is a must-see attraction. Tours of the Athens Lunatic Asylum and graveyard are offered only in the spooky month of October. The asylum is now a part of the Ridges, affiliated with Ohio University and the Kennedy Museum of Art. Throughout the year, rotating art exhibits are on display, but in October, visitors are allowed to tour the asylum and learn of its haunted past.

Tour guides will lead you through the graveyard and the buildings where lobotomies, shock therapy, and hydrotherapy were once the norm. The graveyard holds nearly 2,000 souls, most marked only by a number.

Best Time to Visit: The museum is only open from Wednesday through Saturday, and the only time tours are offered are in October.

Pass/Permit/Fees: Walking tour tickets are $15 per person.

Closest City or Town: Athens

Physical Address: 118 Ridges Cir, Athens, OH 45701

GPS Coordinates: 39.3204° N, 82.1101° W

Did You Know? The first patient at the asylum was a 14-year-old girl with epilepsy.

Battelle Darby Creek Metro Park

There's a lot to see and do at this 7,000-acre park, the largest in central Ohio, but the most popular feature is the herd of bison that roam in two enclosed pastures. The best view of the bison is from either the Darby Creek Greenway Trail or the overlook deck at the Nature Center.

The park also features forests, prairies, and wetlands. You can hike to a creek to splash around, hang a hammock in Hammock Grove, go canoeing or kayaking, or explore miles of trails. The restored Wetland Area offers beautiful views at sunset.

Best Time to Visit: The best time to visit is during the late spring or early summer.

Pass/Permit/Fees: It's free to visit the park.

Closest City or Town: Columbus

Physical Address: 1775 Darby Creek Dr, Galloway, OH 43119

GPS Coordinates: 39.9039° N, 83.2148° W

Did You Know? The park surrounds 13 miles of the Big and Little Darby creeks.

Cornhenge

This isn't the type of corn maze you get lost in. Cornhenge is an art project that showcases Ohio's agricultural roots. Over 109 sculptures, each reaching 6 feet high, dot the park in neat rows, inviting visitors to walk around and through to experience it.

Cornhenge sits in Sam Frantz Park, named after the local man who formerly owned and farmed the land. He worked directly with Ohio State University to create new species of hybrid corn, and the art project is dedicated in his honor, as well as to those who had farmed the land before.

Best Time to Visit: The best time to see Cornhenge is in winter when visitors can play in the snow and build their own white sculptures.

Pass/Permit/Fees: It's free to explore Cornhenge.

Closest City or Town: Columbus

Physical Address: 4995 Rings Rd, Dublin, OH 43017

GPS Coordinates: 40.0852° N, 83.1236° W

Did You Know? One single cob in Cornhenge weighs 1,500 pounds.

Garden of Constants

The Garden of Constants is where math and creativity come to play. This art installation at Ohio State University invites visitors to explore the park and to climb and photograph the copper and bronze number statues.

Some numbers are organized into mathematical formulas in honor of the university's computer and engineering buildings. Other sculptures stand alone and are open to your own interpretation, proving you don't have to be a math whiz to appreciate an equation. A scale replica of the *Steel Teaching Sculpture*, constructed with OSU-red steel, is nearby at Hitchcock Hall.

Best Time to Visit: Visit the garden during the summer when the campus is less crowded.

Pass/Permit/Fees: It's free to explore the Garden of Constants.

Closest City or Town: Columbus

Physical Address: 2055 Millikin Rd, Columbus, OH 43210

GPS Coordinates: 40.0023° N, 83.0163° W

Did You Know? The zero sculpture looks like the Ohio State University logo.

Gates of Hell

Enter at your own risk. The Gates of Hell are marked by the teeth of a graffiti monster, and graffiti lines the walls of the tunnel before it all disappears into pitch blackness. If you can see your way in the dark, a chamber in the center of the tunnel boasts some of the more impressive street murals.

The Gates of Hell is actually a drainage tunnel in Clintonville Park. It earned its ghastly reputation from rumors of a skateboarder who died trying to carve the steep walls. The tunnel is technically closed to the public, but nothing stops explorers from entering at their own risk.

Best Time to Visit: The best time to visit is in the summer.

Pass/Permit/Fees: It's free to enter the Gates of Hell, but do so at your own risk.

Closest City or Town: Columbus

Physical Address: 2754 N High St, Columbus, OH 43202

GPS Coordinates: 40.0184° N, 83.0120° W

Did You Know? At the bottom of the pit is a large drainage tunnel surrounded by a triangular structure that no one knows the use for.

Gavel Sculpture

If you've ever wanted to see the world's largest gavel, it's right here in downtown Columbus outside the Ohio Supreme Court.

Sculpted by Andrew Scott in 2008, the gavel is made of stainless steel and is situated in the middle of a reflecting pool. It's a sight to see when the sun is shining and even prettier at night when the streetlights are on, and the pool lights up.

Explore the pedestrian plaza nearby, which features more sculptures, pools, and fountains situated between the Supreme Court and other city and state judicial buildings.

Best Time to Visit: Avoid the crowds and score free parking when you see the gavel on Saturday or Sunday mornings.

Pass/Permit/Fees: It's free to stop and see the sculpture.

Closest City or Town: Columbus

Physical Address: 145 S Front St, Columbus, OH 43215

GPS Coordinates: 39.9597° N, 83.0022° W

Did You Know? The giant gavel weighs 17,000 pounds or 8.5 tons.

Hayden Falls

Hayden Falls is a hidden gem between a busy street and a suburban neighborhood. Escape from the hustle and bustle by slipping into the Griggs Nature Preserve on Hayden Run Road. A boardwalk and steps lead you to the falls, and an overlook gives you a head-on view of the water.

Pack a picnic and pick a spot at the top of the falls. There are plenty of spots available, and the parking lot near the top of the falls makes it a convenient spot for those who aren't fond of hiking long distances. If you visit after Labor Day, there will be even fewer people on the trail.

The gorge habitat at Hayden Falls is unique to Ohio's Scioto River region and serves as home to endangered plant species. The boardwalk was built to protect this sensitive ecosystem while still giving visitors a chance to see this spectacular natural wonder.

Best Time to Visit: The best time to hike to these falls is in the spring.

Pass/Permit/Fees: It's free to visit the falls.

Closest City or Town: Columbus

Physical Address: 4460 Hayden Run Rd, Columbus, OH 43221

GPS Coordinates: 40.0700° N, 83.1039° W

Did You Know? Keep your eye on the weather. When the water is high, the boardwalk is impassable.

Leatherlips Monument

Chief Shateyaronyah of the Wyandot tribe was known as Leatherlips by white settlers because he never broke a promise. He was a man of his word, and it cost him his life when he signed the Treaty of Greenville in 1795.

This monument was erected in 1990. The limestone slabs rise 12 feet, shaping the chief's face as it looks west toward the Scioto River. The spot where the monument sits is the last-known campsite of Leatherlips, and the Old Leatherlips Monument a few miles north of the sculpture marks his grave.

Visitors can climb to the top of the monument and look out over the same land Chief Shateyaronyah traded to become modern-day Ohio.

Best Time to Visit: The best time to visit is during the fall, when the leaves are changing all around the memorial.

Pass/Permit/Fees: It's free to visit the monument.

Closest City or Town: Columbus

Physical Address: 7377 Riverside Dr, Powell, OH 43065

GPS Coordinates: 40.2889° N, 83.1430° W

Did You Know? Leatherlips's brother ordered his execution.

Lockville Ruins

Before railroads and multi-lane highways, goods and resources moved in and out of Ohio on canals. A remnant of this bygone era—a lock for the O & E Canal—rests in Lockville Park. The water has since dried up, and the sandstone is crumbling, but visitors can climb through the empty channel for a peek into Ohio's past.

A 19th-century covered bridge sits between locks 11 and 12, saved from demolition and moved to the park to bring a little more historical charm to Columbus's urban sprawl.

Lockville Park is one of the smaller parks in Ohio, but there are designated picnic areas and plenty of walking paths for families and dogs to explore the ruins.

Best Time to Visit: The best time to explore the ruins is during the fall.

Pass/Permit/Fees: It's free to visit the park and the ruins.

Closest City or Town: Columbus

Physical Address: Greenfield, Fairfield, Lockville Park, 5895 Pieckerinton Rd NW, Carroll, OH 43112

GPS Coordinates: 39.8204° N, 82.7400° W

Did You Know? The only canals still in use in Ohio are in Muskingum Valley near Zanesville.

The Topiary Park

The Topiary Park is a re-creation of George Seurat's famous painting, *A Sunday Afternoon on the Island of La Grande Jatte*. Visitors can walk among characters from the painting as they sunbathe and picnic.

There are 67 topiaries in the park, featuring people, boats, dogs, a monkey, and a cat. The sculptures, made of yew trees, were fashioned by famous Columbus sculptor James T. Mason.

A walking trail will lead you through the park and around the pond, but feel free to venture off the beaten path to set up a picnic of your own or find your favorite scene from the painting.

Best Time to Visit: The best time to visit is in the spring, when everything is in bloom.

Pass/Permit/Fees: It's free to explore Topiary Park.

Closest City or Town: Columbus

Physical Address: 480 E Town St, Columbus, OH 43215

GPS Coordinates: 39.9611° N, 82.9867° W

Did You Know? Topiary Park is on the grounds of one of the first all-deaf schools in the country. The remaining school structure on site is a designated historical building.

Trap History Museum

All 4,000 animal traps on display in the Trap History Museum are from the personal collection of museum curator Tom Parr, who is the editor of *Trapper's World* magazine. He works directly with Ohio wildlife agencies to humanely capture, tag, and release animals into the wild.

Four rooms in the museum showcase different eras and kinds of trapping, with one exhibit featuring only mouse traps. Other exhibits include modern trapping equipment and various types of fur-trade tools used throughout history.

Parr gives guided tours of the museum and opens the doors to visitors whenever they make an appointment.

Best Time to Visit: Tours are by appointment, and the best time to visit is whenever is convenient to you.

Pass/Permit/Fees: Call the museum to book a tour.

Closest City or Town: Columbus

Physical Address: 6106 Bausch Rd, Galloway, OH 43119

GPS Coordinates: 39.9065° N, 83.1571° W

Did You Know? The most common nuisance animals that Parr helps to capture and release are coyotes.

Greenville Falls

The historic Greenville Falls provided electric power to the farmers of Western Ohio throughout the early 19th century. You'll see the Albery Mill, turbines, and the remnants of the old wooden dam on your way to and from your spot on the falls overlook platform.

The falls themselves are very wide, spreading across the cascade and falling only 20 feet, but the water is gorgeous, and the view of the natural limestone arch carved by the water is perfect.

The possibility of catching sight of rare wildlife is high, so bring your binoculars in the spring for birdwatching and keep your eyes peeled. Pack your lunch, and don't forget your fishing pole. After a short hike to the falls, there are plenty of spots to rest up for lunch or cast a line for a relaxing afternoon.

Best Time to Visit: The best time to visit is the fall for fishing and wildlife sightings.

Pass/Permit/Fees: It's free to see the waterfall.

Closest City or Town: Covington

Physical Address: 9140 Covington-Gettysburg Rd, Covington, OH 45318

GPS Coordinates: 40.1096° N, 84.3759° W

Did You Know? Blue jays, dark-eyed juncos, and northern flickers are the most commonly sighted birds at Greenville Falls.

National Museum of the U.S. Air Force

You'll see plenty of warcraft at this museum, including the last remaining XB-70A Valkyrie, the prototype for the B-70 supersonic fighter jet, and the ill-fated anti-Soviet Avrocar VZ-9AV, but don't assume the National Museum of the U.S. Air Force is nothing but aircraft.

The highlight of the museum is "Stumpy," the heroic messenger pigeon that survived an exploding shell in WWI to deliver his message. The bird was born in the trenches and had a skill for dodging bullets. Unfortunately, he was blown out of the air and lost his leg. The display uses his official name, John Silver, after the one-legged pirate in *Treasure Island*. It's located in the Early Years section, which features other WWI memorabilia.

Best Time to Visit: To avoid the crowds, visit the museum between November and March.

Pass/Permit/Fees: Museum entry is free, and guided tours of the restoration center are available every first and third Friday.

Closest City or Town: Dayton

Physical Address: 1100 Spaatz St, Dayton, OH 45431

GPS Coordinates: 39.7814° N, 84.1106° W

Did You Know? Soldiers stationed at John Silver's Schofield Barracks are forbidden from calling him Stumpy.

Tappan Lake

Water adventure awaits on this 2,350-acre lake. Engines up to 399 horsepower are allowed for wakeboarding, water skiing, and tubing. Boats can be rented at the marina, or you can launch your own boat from one of three public boat ramps.

With 47 miles of beach, Tappan Lake also offers more shoreline fishing than any other lake in Ohio. Catfish, bass, bullheads, and yellow perch are waiting to be caught, and licenses are required for anglers aged 16 or older.

Turkey Ridge Trail (1.2 miles) leads to the wildlife area at Beal Farm and also connects to the statewide Buckeye Trail. Other wildlife and birding hikes include the Deer Trail (3 miles), Fox Trail (3.8 miles), and the Red Fox Trail (2.4 miles).

Best Time to Visit: Visitors will have the most fun at Tappan Lake during the summer.

Pass/Permit/Fees: It's free to swim and hike at the lake, and campsite reservations start at $8.

Closest City or Town: Dover

Physical Address: 84000 Mallarnee Rd., Deersville, OH 44693

GPS Coordinates: 40.3181° N, 81.1866° W

Did You Know? The lake was created when the dam on Little Stillwater Creek was built.

The Ernest Warther Museum & Gardens

Ernest Warther started making his intricate wood carvings in 1913 to document the history of the steam engine, but by 1936, there wasn't enough room in his house for all his creations. He then moved them into a tiny, one-room museum in his back yard, and visitors continue to come from all over.

Today, the museum sits on the edge of Warther's old property, and his granddaughter, Carol Warther-Moreland, directs the museum. The collection features all 64 of Warther's creations, plus the works by his wife, Freida, who mounted more than 70,000 different buttons in different designs. The gardens on the property invite visitors to explore outside the museum as well as inside.

Best Time to Visit: The best time to visit is in spring when the flowers are in bloom.

Pass/Permit/Fees: Entrance fees are $15 per adult, $13.50 per senior, $7 per student, and $5 for children under 11.

Closest City or Town: Dover

Physical Address: 331 Karl Ave, Dover, OH 44622

GPS Coordinates: 40.5257° N, 81.4878° W

Did You Know? Warther's largest carving is 3 feet long, while the smallest is no bigger than half an inch.

Lake Erie

At 6.3 million acres, Lake Erie is just the fourth-largest of the five Great Lakes. There are plenty of ways to access the lake, no matter where you are in the state. Fairport Harbor, Headlands Beach, and Euclid Beach are all commonly visited recreational spots on Lake Erie's coastline.

These family-friendly beaches come with varying accommodations, lifeguards, and concession stands, but nature trails abound for those who want to explore more than the sand.

If getting on the water is your goal, bring or rent a boat to fish, sail, or swim. There are also opportunities to sign up for shipwreck dives; there are believed to be 8,000 wrecks at the bottom of Lake Erie.

Best Time to Visit: The best time to visit Lake Erie is in the summer.

Pass/Permit/Fees: Lake Erie is free to visit, but parking and rental fees can vary at different beaches.

Closest City or Town: Fairport Harbor

Physical Address: Fairport Harbor Lakefront Park, 301 Huntington Beach, Dr, Fairport Harbor, OH 44077

GPS Coordinates: 41.6659° N, 81.4432° W

Did You Know? The frozen lighthouse on the Cleveland coast sometimes ices over so badly that ships cannot see it.

Geneva State Park

No matter what time of year you choose to visit, Geneva State Park will have something for you. It is one of the most popular camping spots in the summer, and in the fall, the park fills with birdwatchers quietly waiting for a sight of Lake Erie's many migratory bird species.

There's an all-natural adventure awaiting anyone who visits the park, and the diversity of Geneva State Park means there is something to enjoy in every season. The sandy shores of the beach are perfect in summer, but the freshwater marshes and the paved hiking trail through the woods are best enjoyed during the fall or winter.

The best time to camp in Ohio is during the fall, but camping is available all year round, with concierge services and lakefront cottages available for those who would rather "glamp" along Lake Erie.

Best Time to Visit: The best time to visit is between September and October.

Pass/Permit/Fees: It's free to visit the park for the day, and campsites start at $30 per night.

Closest City or Town: Geneva

Physical Address: 4499 Padanarum Rd, Geneva, OH 44041

GPS Coordinates: 41.8515° N, 80.9771° W

Did You Know? Rare plants such as sea rockets and beach peas can be found on Geneva State Park beaches.

Leo Petroglyphs State Memorial

The Leo Petroglyphs were carved into the sandstone cliff face by the Fort Ancient peoples, a native tribe of the Ohio River Valley, over 1,000 years ago. The petroglyphs represent over 30 animals and humans, along with a few interesting abstract drawings.

Boasting some of the best-preserved cave drawings in the world, this is a popular site for historians and hikers. You can reach the glyphs via the half-mile trail that starts from Park Road. The trail parallels a creek and a gorge with cliffs that tower more than 20 feet above.

Visitors are welcome to explore the gorge and its several hidden waterfalls, but be respectful of the homes and people who live nearby. The site is designated as a National Historic Landmark, and the state of Ohio maintains the area through the Ohio History Connection.

Best Time to Visit: The best time to explore this historical site is during the spring.

Pass/Permit/Fees: It's free to see the petroglyphs.

Closest City or Town: Jackson

Physical Address: 357 Township Hwy 224, Ray, OH 45672

GPS Coordinates: 39.1505° N, 82.6748° W

Did You Know? It's believed that the tribe that inscribed the petroglyphs also built the Great Serpent Mound.

The Temple of Tolerance

The Temple of Tolerance is in Jim Bowsher's backyard. He built the temple and the surrounding shrines himself over 25 years to create a safe space for people to visit, meditate, or play.

If you visit on the weekends, you're likely to see children playing back there. In some sense, it is a sort of playground. The winding, whimsical paths through the stone folk art seem to lead to nowhere until you end up right at the entrance of the temple.

The rocks in Jim's temple and the surrounding monoliths come from all over, including one from Woodstock and a piece of granite countertop that John Dillinger jumped over.

Best Time to Visit: The best time to visit the temple is in the fall.

Pass/Permit/Fees: It's free to visit the rock garden and temple.

Closest City or Town: Lima

Physical Address: 203 S Wood St., Wapakoneta, OH 45895

GPS Coordinates: 40.5689° N, 84.1848° W

Did You Know? Jim keeps a detailed, cross-referenced list of where each rock came from.

Ash Cave Falls

Ash Cave Falls is a rare sight because it only flows from its 90-foot-high recess during the spring. The early months of spring offer the best chance of seeing the falls in action.

In April, Ash Cave Falls drips from the curved recess of the 700-foot-long cave, but come winter; it becomes a gorgeous ice structure that is breathtaking to see. The combination of winter ice and beach sand in the cave will make you feel like you're at a frozen shore as you explore.

To see more wintry waterfalls, follow the Grandma Gatewood Trail from behind Ash Cave for 3 miles to Cedar Falls, a 50-foot waterfall that freezes into something beautiful for the winter. This guidebook contains a separate entry dedicated entirely to the falls.

Best Time to Visit: The best time to visit is in April to see the falls at their peak or in January for a beautiful winter scene.

Pass/Permit/Fees: It's free to see the falls.

Closest City or Town: Logan

Physical Address: 27291 OH-56, South Bloomingville, OH 43152

GPS Coordinates: 39.3969° N, 82.5457° W

Did You Know? Ash Cave is named after the pile of ashes found in the cave by early settlers.

Boch Hollow State Nature Preserve

Boch Hollow Nature Preserve is a hands-on exploratory experience perfect for children and young families who want to learn more about Ohio's ecosystems. Boch Hollow features wetlands, waterfalls, wildflowers, and hiking trails that connect with the longer Buckeye Trail.

The loop through the preserve covers 7 miles of wilderness that is particularly perfect for birdwatching during the spring and fall migrations. The trail also highlights the unique geological formations of Ohio, from the sandstone to the hidden creeks, ponds, and elusive Corkscrew Falls, which visitors can access only with a permit.

Three more hiking trails are accessible from OH-664, Beach Camp Road, and Bremen Road. From these spots, trailheads start at the parking lot and offer various vantage points throughout one of the newest and most unique preserves in the state.

Best Time to Visit: The best time to visit is in the spring.

Pass/Permit/Fees: It is free to visit the preserve.

Closest City or Town: Logan

Physical Address: 7000 Beach Camp Rd, Logan, OH 43138

GPS Coordinates: 39.6336° N, 82.4239° W

Did You Know? No hunting, fishing, or camping is allowed in Boch Hollow.

Cedar Falls

Another quick hike leads to yet another stupendous waterfall: Cedar Falls in Hocking Hills State Park. Cedar Falls is the same size as Cascade Falls, and reaching it is also only a half-mile hike.

A bonus is the 12-foot waterfall right next to it, called Hidden Falls because it sneaks out from the landscape. The remaining half-mile of the trail leads through rock formations, up natural steps, and over a boardwalk. This Cedar Falls trail is considered moderate and can be crowded during the summer.

Best Time to Visit: The best time to see the falls is during the spring when the wildflowers are in bloom, and the snow is melting. During the late spring and early summer, you may see hikers soaking their feet in the pool beneath the falls, but be aware that swimming and wading are prohibited. To avoid the crowds and see the falls at their peak, visit in late winter or early spring.

Pass/Permit/Fees: It's free to see the falls.

Closest City or Town: Logan

Physical Address: Cedar Falls Trailhead Parking, OH-374 W, Logan, OH 43138

GPS Coordinates: 39.4186° N, 82.5266° W

Did You Know? Early pioneers mistook the hemlock trees for cedars when they named the falls.

Corkscrew Falls

Corkscrew Falls recently opened up to the public. Access to the falls isn't very obvious; you'll have to look for the trailhead marked by ODNR signage off Zwickle Road. From there, it is only a half-mile hike to the 10-foot waterfall.

Not many people have seen Corkscrew Falls, so your hike should be quiet and serene. Listen for the rushing water to tell you that you're close, and take your time when you arrive to really soak in the natural beauty of it all.

To access the falls, follow the footpath off the freeway that parallels the creek and dead-ends at the waterfall. The falls are located within the Boch Hollow State Nature Preserve, a fragile and unique ecosystem that protects an endangered species of clover in Ohio.

Best Time to Visit: Come between March and May to see the water rushing down the falls.

Pass/Permit/Fees: Corkscrew Falls is free to visit, but you'll need a free ODNR permit.

Closest City or Town: Logan

Physical Address: 100001090000, Logan, OH 43138

GPS Coordinates: 39.6329° N, 82.4343° W

Did You Know? Corkscrew Falls is officially known as Robinson Falls.

Hocking Hills State Park

Some of the most famous spots mentioned in this book are found in Hocking Hills State Park, including Old Man's Cave, Cantwell Cliffs, and the Rock House. To see them all, visitors are welcome to camp or lodge in Hocking Hills. Campsites vary from primitive to electric to fully furnished vacation cabins and lodge houses.

The history of Hocking Hills dates back nearly 7,000 years; there is evidence that ancient Adena peoples lived in the caves that dot the hiking trails. Visitors can also see the geological history of Ohio in the sandstone of the cliffs and caves. No matter what time of year you visit, there is always something to see and explore.

Best Time to Visit: Summer is the best month for rock climbing, archery practice, and horseback riding. Spring and fall are the best months for hiking because of the change of seasons. In the winter, visitors will have wonderfully private views of frozen Cedar Falls.

Pass/Permit/Fees: Campsites start at $29 per night.

Closest City or Town: Logan

Physical Address: 19852 OH-664, Logan, OH 43138

GPS Coordinates: 39.4238° N, 82.5379° W

Did You Know? Hocking Hills is based on the Native American word *hockhocking*, which refers to the bottle shape of the valley carved by the river.

Old Man's Cave

There are reasons that Old Man's Cave is one of the most popular hiking destinations in Hocking Hills State Park. It offers up some of the most awe-inspiring views, including epic rock formations, waterfalls, and the haunting Devil's Bathtub that's so deep it's impossible to climb out. The first waterfall on your hike will be Upper Falls, which dribbles down under a man-made stone bridge. The next is Lower Falls, which you can reach by crossing the stone bridge.

If you want to see Broken Rock Falls, keep on the Broken Rock Trail instead of heading down the stone steps to the cave. Old Man's Cave is named for the hermit Richard Rowe, who lived in the recessed cave with his two dogs in 1796. Legend says he is buried beneath the ledge over the main entrance of the cave. Currently, the boardwalk overlook of the recess is right next to the ledge.

Best Time to Visit: The best time to see Old Man's Cave is in the winter.

Pass/Permit/Fees: Hocking Hills State Park is free, and campsites start at $23 per night

Closest City or Town: Logan

Physical Address: 19988 OH-664 Scenic, Logan, OH 43138

GPS Coordinates: 39.4349° N, 82.5418° W

Did You Know? Two other former residents of the cave, brothers Nathaniel and Pat Rayon, are buried nearby.

Paul A. Johnson Pencil Sharpener Museum

Rev. Paul A. Johnson grew his pencil sharpener collection for over 20 years. It started when his wife gave him car-shaped sharpeners in the 1980s, and he collected over 3,000 different sharpeners before his death in 2010.

His Pencil Sharpener Museum is the largest collection in the United States and features every design imaginable, from famous cartoon characters to the old shelf-mounted sharpeners you see in libraries and schools.

When Rev. Johnson requested that the collection stay together, the Hocking Hills Tourism agency moved the entire collection to the Hocking Hills Regional Welcome Center.

Best Time to Visit: The best time to visit the museum and Hocking Hills is in the winter.

Pass/Permit/Fees: The museum is free.

Closest City or Town: Logan

Physical Address: 13178 OH-664, Logan, OH 43138

GPS Coordinates: 39.5365° N, 82.4446° W

Did You Know? The collection began in Rev. Johnson's office before moving to the shed in the family's backyard.

The Rock House

This is the only true cave in Hocking Hills, but it is really a 200-foot-long tunneled corridor carved 150 feet up in the sandstone cliffs. Its widest point is about 30 feet, and the ceilings can reach up to 25 feet. You can reach the cave via the Rock House Trail (1 mile).

The history of Rock House dates back to prehistoric times when ancient tribes used the cave for shelter and cooking. Hike through the small recesses and rooms in the back of the cave to see where small fires turned these tiny spaces into baking ovens. There is also a man-made trough carved into the stone to catch rainwater.

The numerous carvings in the cave walls are a testament to the history of Rock House, from modern calligraphy to old adages. There are even carvings left behind by robbers and thieves who used the space as a hideout during the 18th and 19th centuries.

Best Time to Visit: The best time to hike to Rock House is between August and November.

Pass/Permit/Fees: It's free to visit Hocking Hills State Park, and campsites start at $29 per night.

Closest City or Town: Logan

Physical Address: 16350 OH-374, Laurelville, OH 43135

GPS Coordinates: 39.4983° N, 82.6171° W

Did You Know? In 1835, Rock House featured a new hotel, stable, and post office.

President Warren G. Harding's Tomb

This tomb is the last of the elaborate memorials that were so popular during the early 1900s. It resembles a circular Greek temple and features iconic Doric columns made of Georgian white marble. Inside are the graves of Harding and the first lady. Harding served only two years before dying in office, and his presidency was known for its corruption.

The accusation of bribery among his cabinet is said to have cost him his life, and the tomb almost wasn't finished due to his tarnished reputation. It wasn't until 1931, when then-president Herbert Hoover dedicated the tomb, that it was officially recognized as a historic site.

Best Time to Visit: The best time to visit the memorial is in the spring.

Pass/Permit/Fees: It's free to visit the memorial and nearby Veterans Memorial Park.

Closest City or Town: Marion

Physical Address: 966-870 Delaware Ave, Marion, OH 43302

GPS Coordinates: 40.5735° N, 83.1229° W

Did You Know? The tomb doesn't have a roof because the president wished to be buried outside, so the memorial remains open to the air and is covered with ivy.

Lake Hope

Lake Hope is tucked neatly among the woods of Zaleski State Forest in the Big Sandy Run valley. Swimming is allowed near the dam, and the lake is open for ice fishing in the winter. The cliffs surrounding the lake showcase the history of the region, with its abandoned mines, old iron smelters, and ancient mounds waiting to be explored.

Hiking trails here are graded moderate to difficult because of the steep and rugged terrain, but young families and novice hikers can still enjoy the short Buzzard Cave Trail (0.5 miles), starting at Hope Furnace and leading to one of the most interesting caves in the region. Peninsula Trail (3 miles) is a little tougher. For more historical hikes, take the Hope Furnace Trail (3.2 miles) to the Keeton Cemetery or follow the Old Hollows Trail (1.5 miles), which starts at the Zaleski Backpacking trailhead and leads to an old pioneer cemetery.

Best Time to Visit: The best time to visit the lake is between April and October.

Pass/Permit/Fees: It's free to hike and swim at the lake, and campsites start at $20 per night.

Closest City or Town: Athens

Physical Address: Lake Hope State Park, 27331 OH-278, McArthur, OH 45651

GPS Coordinates: 39.3293° N, 82.3567° W

Did You Know? During the summer, visitors can feed hummingbirds at the nature center.

Zaleski State Forest

It would take you as long as three days to hike every trail and loop in Zaleski State Forest. The Zaleski Loop backpacking trails are the longest in the park, with a combined distance of nearly 30 miles. South Loop is the shorter of the two (11.3 miles) and leads to a variety of campsites. North Loop is longer (19.5 miles) and more overgrown, and it includes a few caves. For a less strenuous hike, take the Moonville Tunnel Rail Trail (1.2 miles). The old railroad is one of the last remnants proving that the ghost town of Moonville once existed in the forest, and many visitors claim to see the ghosts of fallen miners at night shining their lanterns in the tunnel. The trailheads for the tunnel start at Raccoon Creek, but backpackers will want to catch the longer loop trailheads at Hope Furnace, an old iron smelting furnace that once produced ammunition and weapons for the Union Army during the Civil War.

Best Time to Visit: The best time to see Zaleski State Forest is early summer, between May and June.

Pass/Permit/Fees: It's free to visit the forest, and campsites are first-come, first-served.

Closest City or Town: Athens

Physical Address: 27331 OH-278, Macarthur, OH 45651.

GPS Coordinates: 39.3558° N, 82.3387° W

Did You Know? Zaleski is the second-largest forest in Ohio.

Chippewa Lake

Chippewa Lake is a gem hidden right outside Akron. Take a few steps from the parking lot, and you'll be in the serene wilderness around the lake. Hiking farther into the region will inspire more thoughts of relaxation, and you might just stop to meditate right then and there. The Medina County Park District is in the process of restoring some of the wetlands and marshes around the lake, and the new public boat launch gives visitors a chance to explore the water by kayak, canoe, or paddleboat. The Chippewa Rail Trail (5 miles) is the easiest way to see the lake and surrounding wilderness by foot.

Best Time to Visit: During the fall, this area bursts with bright oranges and reds that contrast vividly with the bright blue Ohio sky. Keep your eyes on the skies for a chance to see a bald eagle.

Pass/Permit/Fees: Campsites start at $34-$40 per night.

Closest City or Town: Medina

Physical Address: Chippewa Rail Trail parking lot, Chippewa Rd, Chippewa Lake, OH 44215

GPS Coordinates: 41.07711° N, 81.89404° W

Did You Know? You can see the skeletons of the rides left behind by the abandoned Chippewa Lake Amusement Park from the trail.

Findley Lake

Findley Lake was once a state forest and remains heavily wooded with local pines to this day. Hikers can hop onto the statewide Buckeye Trail from here or choose from any of the shorter trails around the water. The loop around the lake is 3.3 miles and poorly marked in some areas, so be prepared with offline maps. Thorn Mountain Bike Trail at Findley Lake is a favorite in the state and accommodates bikers of all levels.

The trail is relatively flat on its way to the campgrounds but snakes through the wood, with steep slopes, sharp turns, and winding sections, which make for an exciting ride for more experienced bikers. The bike trail connects with the Buckeye Trail. Youngsters and families will enjoy a hike on Storybook Trail, exploring both the state forest and favorite childhood stories along a half-mile stone path. A free little library is located at the start of the trail where visitors can take a book home or leave one behind for the next hiker.

Best Time to Visit: Fall is the best time of year to hike.

Pass/Permit/Fees: Campsite fees start at $40 per night.

Closest City or Town: Medina

Physical Address: Findley State Park, 25381 OH-58, Wellington, OH 44090

GPS Coordinates: 41.1323° N, 82.2115° W

Did You Know? Findley Lake is a sanctuary for the endangered Dukes' skipper butterfly.

Headlands Beach

Headlands Beach is one of a kind. Not only is it the longest beach in the state, but it's also home to some of the rarest plants and wildlife in the country. The unique combination of sand, surf, and sunshine create sand dunes that are home to beach peas and purple sand grass. The area also has bald eagle nests, red fox dens, and more.

Visitors can take the Buckeye Trail (1.5 miles) to the Headlands Dunes State Nature Preserve for a closer look at flora and fauna. The trail runs the length of the beach and leads to various picnic areas throughout the park.

Best Time to Visit: The best time to visit is during the warm months for swimming and the monarch butterfly migration. Headlands Beach remains open to visitors during the winter. Swimming isn't allowed during the winter months, but the hills near the beach are perfect for sledding and cross-country skiing along Buckeye Trail.

Pass/Permit/Fees: It's free to visit the beach all year long.

Closest City or Town: Mentor

Physical Address: 9601 Headlands Rd, Mentor, OH 44060

GPS Coordinates: 41.7576° N, 81.28723° W

Did You Know? Headlands Beach is a topless beach.

Ariel-Foundation Park

This is more than just an outdoor space. There is something for everyone, even those who aren't keen on exploring the outdoors. Park visitors are encouraged to tour the museum, climb the observation tower, and explore the ruins of an old glass-making factory.

For outdoor enthusiasts, lakes and walking paths abound, with beautiful steel sculptures throughout to inspire the mind as well as the body. Kayaks, canoes, and fishing are allowed on the lakes, and hiking trails vary in length between 0.5 and 1.25 miles. Hiking trails at Ariel-Foundation connect with the Kokosing Gap Trail and the Heart of Ohio Trail.

Best Time to Visit: The best time to visit and hike the park is during the fall.

Pass/Permit/Fees: It's free to visit the park.

Closest City or Town: Mt. Vernon

Physical Address: 10 Pittsburgh Ave, Mt Vernon, OH 43050

GPS Coordinates: 40.3824° N, 82.4951° W

Did You Know? Ariel Corporation is a major manufacturing company in Ohio and owner of the original glass company.

Cascade Falls

You don't have to be an experienced hiker to see one of the most beautiful waterfalls in Ohio. Cascade Falls is at the end of a short half-mile hike through Nelson Kennedy Ledges State Park that leads you by unique rock formations and to secret waterfalls.

To reach Cascade Falls, follow the Yellow Trail across a wooden boardwalk. Even though it's one of the shortest hikes in the state, it gives hikers three unique views of the falls. A recessed cave on the trail is one vantage point from beneath the waterfall, and the path also leads behind the falls and all the way up to the top.

Although it's a short hike, you'll still have a chance to climb through rock formations and explore caves, including the Devil's Icebox and Old Maid's Kitchen.

Best Time to Visit: It's best to visit during the spring or winter.

Pass/Permit/Fees: It's free to hike to the falls.

Closest City or Town: Nelson

Physical Address: 12440 OH-282, Garrettsville, OH 44231

GPS Coordinates: 41.3299° N, 81.0409° W

Did You Know? You will have to crawl on your hands and knees through Dwarf Man's Pass to reach the falls.

Nelson Kennedy Ledges State Park

Don't let the bizarre names of the rock formations in Nelson Kennedy Ledges State Park deter you. It is one of the few places in the country where you can still climb among the boulders, and the Devil's Icebox and Old Maid's Kitchen are worth the hike.

Hikers of all skill levels will find a trail at Nelson Kennedy. The White Trail (1 mile) is the longest and easiest hike in the park, with plenty of rocks to climb on and a waterfall to see. To reach the Devil's Icebox, which is a very tight squeeze to a cool cave, take the Cascade Falls loop trail (2 miles) marked in yellow.

Nearby, Nelson Ledges Quarry Park is open in the summer for swimming and events. Costs vary depending on the season and whether or not there is a festival.

Best Time to Visit: The best time to climb the rocks is between August and October.

Pass/Permit/Fees: It's free to visit Nelson Ledges. Camping costs $20 per night for each adult and $10 per night for each child.

Closest City or Town: Nelson

Physical Address: 12440 OH-282, Garrettsville, OH 44231

GPS Coordinates: 41.3286° N, 81.0387° W

Did You Know? The beaches at Nelson Kennedy are only open if the temperature reaches 70°F or higher.

Buckeye Lake State Park

Buckeye Lake State Park is the oldest state park in Ohio. The lake originally fed the Ohio & Erie Canal system and continues to be a favorite weekend getaway for locals and tourists. Boating, swimming, fishing, and picnics are among the most popular activities at the lake, and hunters can take to the lake and try their shot at waterfowl during the appropriate seasons. Buckeye Lake draws visitors all year long. In the winter, the lake opens up for ice skating and ice fishing, and the flora along the hiking trails blooms beautifully in the spring and changes colors in the fall. Mountain bikers will love the Buckeye Scenic Trail (11 miles) that starts in Heath and weaves down to the lake. Across the lake is the Cranberry Bog State Nature Preserve, one of the last remnants of the original water system that existed before the canal. It is also one of the few remaining pieces of ancient Ohio waterways. Visitors are welcome to explore the area and the visitor center to learn more.

Best Time to Visit: The best time to visit is in the summer when the weather is warm enough for activities on the lake.

Pass/Permit/Fees: The lake is free to visit, and camping fees start at $60 per day.

Closest City or Town: Newark

Physical Address: 2905 Leibs Island Rd NE, Millersport, OH 43046

GPS Coordinates: 39.9082° N, 82.5247° W

Did You Know? Buckeye Lake wasn't big enough to supply the canal, so it was enlarged in the mid-1800s.

Cuyahoga Valley National Park

Hop on the 21-mile Ohio and Erie Canal Towpath Trail in Cuyahoga Valley National Park for a unique hike that showcases the natural and social history of Ohio. Lands that were originally used by the Lenapé Nation became a link to one of the most influential canals in American history. The towpath trail follows the original tugboat canals from Independence through Akron, connecting hikers with visitor centers and a farmers market along the way.

If you'd rather rest your feet, enjoy the views from your seat on a historic train. Scenic tour rides are offered seasonally, and visitors can hop on at any of the park's eight stations. Visitors can also grab their own pair of wheels and hit the East Rim Trail System for four different mountain-biking trails. Each is considered moderate, but East Rim is less technical than Lamb Loop, Post Line, or Edson Run.

Best Time to Visit: The best time to visit is between April and May.

Pass/Permit/Fees: It's free to visit the park.

Closest City or Town: Parma

Physical Address: Valley View, Ohio & Erie Canal Towpath Trail, Valley View, OH 44125

GPS Coordinates: 41.2808° N, 81.5678° W

Did You Know? Cuyahoga is home to seven different species of bats.

Mineral Spring Lake

Mineral Spring Lake Resort combines modern amenities with the nostalgic and authentic experience of primitive camping. The beautiful spring-fed lake is ideal for any boat, kayak, or canoe, and the beaches boast an inflatable water park right on the water for kids of all ages.

The resort spans over 500 acres, and the lake itself is over 100 acres, so get ready to explore and swim. Rent a golf cart, bring a tent, or drive your RV right up to any of the 400 campgrounds equipped with hookups and more.

Take advantage of over 250 acres of ATV trails, or bring your fishing pole and rent a canoe before hitting the water. An on-site snack bar and store will keep you stocked with supplies, whether you're staying for the day or a month, and year-long campsites are available for visitors with the right equipment.

Best Time to Visit: The best time to swim in the lake is in the summer.

Pass/Permit/Fees: Daily passes are $7 per person. The cost for camping varies by site.

Closest City or Town: Peebles

Physical Address: 160 Bluegill Rd, Peebles, OH 45660

GPS Coordinates: 38.9179° N, 83.3731° W

Did You Know? Permanent campers are welcome at the resort, so Mineral Lake will feel more like a community than a campground.

The Great Serpent Mound

The Great Serpent Mound is the largest serpent effigy in the world at 1,300 feet long. It coils through the Ohio countryside in a shape that may be aligned with Earth's solstice and equinox events.

Strangely enough, while most raised mounds of this kind contain burials and other artifacts, there are none in the Great Serpent, leaving academics and locals to debate the age and cultural origin of the mound.

Although we don't know where it came from, the shape of the snake is unmistakable—from the open jaws in the east to the spiraled tail in the west, pointing at the winter solstice sunrise. The nearby Serpent Mound Museum shows how the mound was built.

Best Time to Visit: The best time to visit is between March and May when everything is in bloom, and the park is at its greenest.

Pass/Permit/Fees: It costs $8 per vehicle to enter the park.

Closest City or Town: Peebles

Physical Address: 3850 OH-73, Peebles, OH 45660

GPS Coordinates: 39.0255° N, 83.4302° W

Did You Know? UNESCO is currently considering the Great Serpent Mound as a potential addition to the World Heritage List.

Blue Hen Falls

Blue Hen Falls is one of the most popular waterfalls in Cuyahoga Valley National Park. The trail to the falls is a 3-mile hike that follows the Buckeye Trail and crosses Boston Mill Road. A flight of stairs awaits to lead you to the 15-foot waterfall.

The trail continues past Blue Hen to Buttermilk Falls. The path covers quite a few hills and is not recommended for inexperienced hikers. The trails to the falls recently went through some major repairs and construction due to the amount of foot traffic to the waterfall, and you may have to adjust your hike to access Blue Hen Falls.

Best Time to Visit: If you visit during the fall or winter months, you'll avoid the crowds that fill the park during the spring. You can also truly appreciate the view of Blue Hen Falls when it freezes over in the winter.

Pass/Permit/Fees: It's free to see the falls.

Closest City or Town: Peninsula

Physical Address: Buckeye Trailhead, Wildlife Woods Park, 313 Boston Mills Rd, Peninsula, OH 44264

GPS Coordinates: 41.2597° N, 81.5729° W

Did You Know? Blue Hen Falls is believed to be haunted, and visitors often capture blue orbs when taking photos of the waterfall.

Mohican-Memorial State Forest

What's your favorite season? The Mohican-Memorial State Forest is perfect in all of them. Over 30 miles of hiking trails beckon to visitors all year, and 8 miles of snowmobile trails open up during the winter. Horseback riders have 22 miles of trails to explore, and mountain biking trails span over 24 miles through the trees. When the Ohio Division of Forestry acquired the land in the 1930s, they planted millions of trees to rejuvenate the land and forest, including pines, hemlocks, and oaks.

Take the climb to the top of the 80-foot Mohican Fire Tower for a sweeping 10-mile view above the trees. Get up close and personal on the interactive Discovery Forest Trail (1.5 miles). Learn more about the types of trees in the forest and the forest management techniques used by the Forestry Division. Placards note where and when rows have been cut.

Best Time to Visit: Visit February through June for the best views.

Pass/Permit/Fees: The state forest is free to visit, and campsites start at $25 per day.

Closest City or Town: Perrysville

Physical Address: 975 O D N R Mohican Rd 51, Perrysville, OH 44864

GPS Coordinates: 40.6049° N, 82.2969° W

Did You Know? Over 200 acres of the forest are dedicated to fallen Ohio soldiers at the Memorial Forest Park Shrine.

Catawba Island State Park

Spend the day on the shores of Lake Erie or get right into the water. Swimming is allowed at Catawba Island State Park, although wading is more common because lifeguards aren't present. There are four ramps for launching larger boats and cobblestone beaches where you can launch your kayak or canoe.

Fishing is allowed (with a proper license), and you can catch perch, bass, and catfish from the pier or in the comfort of your own boat. Don't forget to pack warm clothes for a day of ice fishing if you plan on visiting during the winter months.

Visitors are not allowed to camp, but packing a picnic should be on your to-do list. Take a walk around the lake, see the sunset, and bring your binoculars if you have a birdwatcher in your group.

Best Time to Visit: The best time to enjoy the water is between July and September.

Pass/Permit/Fees: $6 per adult, $3.75 per child under 16 years

Closest City or Town: Port Clinton

Physical Address: 4049 E Moores Dock Rd, Port Clinton, OH 43452

GPS Coordinates: 41.5738° N, 82.8562° W

Did You Know? Catawba Island isn't really an island at all.

Perry's Victory and International Peace Memorial

Oliver Hazard Perry led the U.S. Navy to victory during the decisive Battle of Put-in-Bay, solidifying American control of Lake Erie against the British and Spanish during the War of 1812. His memorial stands on South Bass Island as the highest Doric column in the world.

The Peace Memorial opened in 1915 and stands at 352 feet high. It hosts a commemoration of the battle every year in September, and you are welcome to climb 37 steps to the top of the column, where a park ranger will lead you to an elevator that takes you to the very top.

Best Time to Visit: The best time to see the memorial is in August or September.

Pass/Permit/Fees: It's free to visit the memorial, and adults 16 and older can pay $10 to ride the elevator to the viewing deck at the top of the memorial.

Closest City or Town: Port Clinton

Physical Address: 93 Delaware Ave, Put-In-Bay, OH 43456

GPS Coordinates: 41.6545° N, 82.8113° W

Did You Know? The Peace Memorial is taller than the Statue of Liberty.

Shawnee State Forest

Shawnee State Forest is a naturalist's dream. Backpacking trails take hikers to primitive campsites where visitors are welcome to hunt and fish during the appropriate seasons. One of the shorter trails is the Backpack Trailhead to Camp 7, a 10-mile hike with a 1,300-foot elevation gain that leads to a lake and a campsite. Other backpacking trails exceed 30 miles, with shorter side trails that lead to more campsites and add a few extra miles, depending on where you decide to stay.

If you get lost, remember that the main trail is blazed with orange markers while the side trails are marked with white. Keep an eye out for wildlife on the trails. The forest is home to a variety of creatures, from bobcats and black bears to rattlesnakes, butterflies, and lizards. Be alert and remember to check your belongings and properly store food when you're camping to prevent any surprises.

Best Time to Visit: The best time to visit and camp in Shawnee is during the fall.

Pass/Permit/Fees: The state forest is free to visit, and campsites start at $35 per night.

Closest City or Town: Portsmouth

Physical Address: 13291 US-52, West Portsmouth, OH 45663

GPS Coordinates: 38.7096° N, 83.0918° W

Did You Know? The forest was originally used as hunting grounds by the Shawnee tribe.

Cantwell Cliffs

Hiking to Cantwell Cliffs is not for the faint of heart. The trail to the cliffs is strenuous, which discourages many everyday tourists from visiting the spot. This makes it an ideal site for experienced hikers and adventurers who are looking for a quiet spot to sneak away.

The 2-mile trail to the cliffs has only one way in and one way out but provides one of the most unique outdoor experiences in Ohio. While the rim trail offers views from atop the falls, the valley trail takes hikers through the narrow passageways on the towering cliffs.

This is the most remote of all the trails in Hocking Hills, and hikers are required to stay on the marked path for their safety. The trail passes over many narrow blocks and steps with steep elevation changes along the way. Swimming is prohibited, but dogs are allowed on the trail as long as they remain on a leash.

Best Time to Visit: Winter is the best time to visit.

Pass/Permit/Fees: It's free to visit the cliffs. Camping starts at $30–$35 per night.

Closest City or Town: Rockbridge

Physical Address: OH-374, Rockbridge, OH 43149

GPS Coordinates: 39.5400° N, 82.5759° W

Did You Know? The Cantwell Cliffs are almost 150 feet high.

Conkle's Hollow State Nature Park

Be humbled by the 200-foot cliff face at Conkle's Hollow State Nature Park. The gorge itself is only 100 feet wide at certain points, but it's considered the deepest in Ohio. Visitors can explore the gorge via two hiking trails: Lower Trail (0.75 miles) and Upper Trail (2 miles).

Lower Trail is an easy, wheelchair-accessible path. It leads to a boardwalk and several recessed caves that are waiting to be explored. More experienced hikers can use the Upper Trail for the breathtaking views of the cliffs and nature park below.

Upper Trail is a one-way trip that takes hikers to the rim of the cliffs and circles the gorge, offering dizzying views of the nature park below. Some steps are extremely steep, and parts of the trail are very narrow, so exercise extreme caution if you choose the Upper Trail.

Best Time to Visit: The best time to visit the nature park is during the fall.

Pass/Permit/Fees: It's free to visit all year long.

Closest City or Town: Rockbridge

Physical Address: 24858 Big Pine Rd, Rockbridge, OH 43149

GPS Coordinates: 39.4570° N, 82.5764° W

Did You Know? Folk legends tell of money and treasure hidden in the west gorge wall, marked by an ancient petroglyph… if you can find it.

Cedar Point Shores

Cedar Point Shores waterpark stretches along 18 acres of Lake Erie's shoreline, featuring the lake's mythical monster Lemmy and a 5-story water slide that plunges you into complete darkness.

 Families can relax in Cedar Creek or test their skills on the lily pads before battling the waves in Breakwater Bay. The waterpark offers multiple areas for swimmers of all levels and slides for children who aren't quite tall enough for Point Plummet.

Grab your mats and race down the Riptide Raceway to see who is truly the fastest in the park, or grab a tube and brave the rapids on the Runaway lazy river. If you're looking for more thrills, Cedar Point's 18 rollercoasters are right next door, which you can see from your cabana at Lemmy's Lagoon. Resort packages are available to give visitors access to both parks.

Best Time to Visit: It's best to visit on weekdays during May and June when it's less crowded.

Pass/Permit/Fees: Passes start at $29/day.

Closest City or Town: Sandusky

Physical Address: 1 Cedar Point Dr, Sandusky, OH 44870

GPS Coordinates: 41.4879° N, 82.6870° W

Did You Know? Cedar Point Shores was known as Soak City until 2016.

Kelleys Island Glacial Grooves

The glacial grooves on Kelleys Island were carved by the melting Ice Age glacier that created the Great Lakes. It is the largest and most accessible geological fossil in the world, and visitors today can explore the area in search of marine fossils dating back 400 million years.

Natural phenomena abound at Kelleys Island, and the North Pond Trail (1 mile) takes visitors through the flora and fauna that is unique to Ohio. Camping accommodations range from primitive to camper cabins, including two furnished yurts.

Campsites on the island offer the most spectacular views of Lake Erie, with easy access to the shoreline for swimming, fishing, boating, and more. Guests are invited to stay during the winter months as well for ice fishing and cross-country skiing.

Best Time to Visit: It is best to visit during the summer.

Pass/Permit/Fees: Ferry tickets to Kelleys Island are $9 per child and $11 per adult.

Closest City or Town: Sandusky

Physical Address: Kelleys Island Historical Association, 224 Division St, Kelleys Island, OH 43438

GPS Coordinates: 41.6163° N, 82.7065° W

Did You Know? The monarch butterfly fall migration passes through Kelleys Island.

Kelleys Island Wine Company Cellars

Kelleys Island Winery built its first cellar in 1872 when the Midwest was the center of American wines. Ohio's climate and location make it perfect for growing grapes, and local vintners came together to create the Kelleys Island Wine Company cooperative.

The winery processed grapes from all across the state before the Civil War, Prohibition, and accidental fires took their toll. The ruins left behind are on the southwest side of the island, and you will need to take the ferry. The ruins are on private property, but you can access a path off Sunset Road.

Best Time to Visit: The best time to see the ruins is between May and October, but look out for poison ivy.

Pass/Permit/Fees: There is no cover fee, but food and drinks will cost depending on purchase choice.

Closest City or Town: Sandusky

Physical Address: 418 Woodford Rd, Kelleys Island, OH 43438

GPS Coordinates: 41.5955° N, 82.6969° W

Did You Know? In its prime, the winery processed 350,000 gallons of wine per year.

Merry-Go-Round Museum

Carousels were originally made for adults. They went too fast for children at nearly 9 miles per hour, so hold on tight for your ride at the Merry-Go-Round Museum.

Housed in a round building that was once a post office, the Merry-Go-Round Museum features hand-carved wooden carousel frames, scenery panels, animals, and more. Exhibits include the woodcarving shop where some of these pieces were created.

The Allan Herschell carousel you can ride was originally built in 1939 and refurbished in 1991 with animals hand-carved in the museum and others added from carousels from around the world.

Best Time to Visit: The best time to visit the museum is in September or October.

Pass/Permit/Fees: Adults are $6, and seniors are $5. Children are $4. The entrance fee includes a carousel ride.

Closest City or Town: Sandusky

Physical Address: 301 Jackson St, Sandusky, OH 44870

GPS Coordinates: 41.4542° N, 82.7127° W

Did You Know? The oldest carousel in the country is The Flying Horse in Rhode Island.

Seneca Lake Park

While the beach is open only from Memorial Day to Labor Day, the campgrounds, hiking trails, and fishing holes at Seneca Lake Park remain open all year long. The statewide Buckeye Trail crosses through here, and hikers can access it from the Cemetery Trail or the Beech Tree Ridge Trail.

Throughout the summer, the lake is open to swimmers, boats, and jet skis. Engines up to 399 horsepower are allowed on the lake, meaning jet skiers and speedboats can get some serious air, and the full-service marina offers everything a boat needs, from fuel to docking and even sales and rentals.

During the winter, ice fishing is welcome on Senecaville Lake, but anglers can cast a line for catfish, bass, walleye, crappie, and yellow perch during any season.

Best Time to Visit: The park is open year-round, and the best time to visit is between April and October.

Pass/Permit/Fees: Seneca Lake is free to visit, and campsites start at $35 per night.

Closest City or Town: Senecaville

Physical Address: 22172 Park Rd, Senecaville, OH 43780

GPS Coordinates: 39.9057° N, 81.4218° W

Did You Know? There is a fish hatchery located just below the Senecaville Dam.

Charleston Falls

One of the tallest waterfalls in Ohio, Charleston Falls, is worth the hike. It may not be the most dramatic waterfall you see in the state, but it is one of the few that runs year-round. Even during the winter, hikers can enjoy the sound of a waterfall crashing into an ice-cold pool. Charleston Falls Loop is a 1.8-mile gravel trail leading directly to the waterfall, and hikers are welcome to explore the cave nearby. Take the stairs to the top of the falls for scenic views, and then continue on a beautiful hike through the prairie landscape. During the spring, the wildflowers bloom and dot the trail with bright colors and beautiful petals, and the falls will be at their strongest after the winter melt. However, a winter hike will mean fewer people on the trail and more space to enjoy the landscape.

Best Time to Visit: The best time to see the falls is during April and May.

Pass/Permit/Fees: It's free to visit the falls. To host an event, such as a wedding or a photo shoot, a permit is required, which is received from Miami County Park District.

Closest City or Town: Tipp City

Physical Address: 2535 Ross Rd, Tipp City, OH 45371

GPS Coordinates: 39.9184° N, 84.1477° W

Did You Know? If the falls look familiar, it's because Charleston Falls has the same rock strata as Niagara Falls, just on a smaller scale.

Hartman Rock Garden

When Ben Hartman was laid off during the Great Depression, he decided to fill his time building a concrete fish pond on his property. That fish pond became the rock garden you can visit today. Hartman Rock Garden is an outdoor collection of folk art and sculptures made by Hartman himself, including a 7-foot Tree of Life made of red granite and mixed stone.

Other featured folk art includes miniatures of famous homes (including the White House), Noah's Ark, and the Liberty Bell. After Ben died, his wife maintained the garden for 60 years, planting a variety of flowers among Ben's sculptures. The garden is now maintained by the Kohler Foundation.

Best Time to Visit: The best time to see the garden is during the spring when the flowers are in bloom.

Pass/Permit/Fees: It's free to visit the garden.

Closest City or Town: Springfield

Physical Address: 1905 Russell Ave, Springfield, OH 45506

GPS Coordinates: 39.9051° N, 83.8325° W

Did You Know? If you look inside Hartman's sculptures, you'll see tiny figures made of pebbles.

Kiser Lake

Kiser Lake has a 300-foot beach where you can get your feet wet or rent a boat or kayak from the nearby marina. Cast a fishing line from any of the five piers, or try your hand at ice fishing and iceboating in the winter.

Five hiking trails are open to explorers; the Marina Trail is the shortest and the easiest. More experienced hikers can take the Red Oak Trail (1.5 miles) through to the campgrounds, but fallen trees may obstruct the path. The trail is marked with yellow blazes.

If you plan to camp at Kiser Lake, designated campgrounds feature primitive or electric hookups. Visitors can also choose to stay in camper cabins, and group camping opportunities are available by reservation.

Best Time to Visit: August and September are the best months for swimming, hiking, and camping.

Pass/Permit/Fees: Campsites range from $30–$55 per night.

Closest City or Town: Springfield

Physical Address: Kiser Lake State Park 4889 OH-235, Conover, OH 45317

GPS Coordinates: 40.1982° N, 83.9815° W

Did You Know? When the dam was abandoned, John Kiser sold the lake to the state to turn it into the recreational park you can visit today.

Piatt Castles

These are two late-19th-century homes built by brothers Donn and Abram Piatt. Mac-O-Chee, Donn's home, is the bigger of the two. Both mansions boast painted ceilings, intricate woodwork, and iconic Gothic-style dormers.

Both castles also feature some of the first indoor bathrooms of the century, which was a rarity at the time. But only Mac-A-Cheek, Abram's castle, contains his son William McCoy Piatt's curiosity cabinet, which houses unique collectibles and artifacts of the era.

As of today, only Mac-A-Cheek is open to the public for tours and events, and visitors can explore the curiosity cabinet and its historical documents by appointment.

Best Time to Visit: The best time to visit is on the weekends during September and October.

Pass/Permit/Fees: Entrance fees are $13 per adult and $11 per senior. Children ages 15 and under are $7.

Closest City or Town: Springfield

Physical Address: 10051 Township Rd. 47, West Liberty, OH 43357

GPS Coordinates: 40.2514° N, 83.7269° W

Did You Know? Castle Mac-a-Cheek has a secret underground tunnel.

Oak Openings Preserve Metropark

Oak Openings is the largest metropark in Ohio, spanning 5,000 acres of unique wetlands and oak forests. The ecosystem is exceptionally diverse at Oak Openings and a must-see for any nature lover. The park includes dunes, marshes, wetlands, primitive campgrounds, and stick-straight rows of pine trees stretching for miles.

It's quite a sight to see pine trees that were planted in such straight rows, and visitors are known to pick a spot to hang a hammock and lay back to soak in the view. If you'd rather explore, there are over 70 miles of trails, including horseback-riding trails and a singletrack bike path.

Best Time to Visit: Spring is your time to spy bluebirds, lark sparrows, bald eagles, and whippoorwills.

Pass/Permit/Fees: It's free to visit the metropark, and campsites start at $20 per night.

Closest City or Town: Swanton

Physical Address: 4139 Girdham Rd, Swanton, OH 43558

GPS Coordinates: 41.5495° N, 83.8536° W

Did You Know? Oak Openings is home to the endangered Karner blue butterfly and more than one-third of the rarest creatures in Ohio.

Hell Hollow Wilderness Area

There's a reason they call it Hell Hollow. The 262-step trek down to the ravine is nothing compared to the climb back up those stairs. Fortunately, for experienced hikers, Hell Hollow Wilderness Area is an off-trail explorer's dream. There are more than 800 acres to explore and at least 12 waterfalls scattered throughout, just waiting to be found.

The most popular trail to Hell Hollow is Beechridge Loop. It's only 1 mile long, but you must climb the stairwell that earned the park its name. Hidden Lake Loop is another mile-long trail, but it's an easy loop around the water that includes fishing spots, a wildflower meadow, and an archery range. If you venture off-trail, be prepared to meet some friendly wildlife on your way, including rabbits, herons, and a few turtles if you're lucky.

Best Time to Visit: The best time to visit is between October and May.

Pass/Permit/Fees: It's free to visit Hell Hollow, and camping starts at $10 per night.

Closest City or Town: Thompson

Physical Address: Leroy Center Rd, Leroy Township, OH 44077

GPS Coordinates: 41.6896° N, 81.1186° W

Did You Know? You can skip the stairs and take the path to Little Known Falls, which starts at the base of the stairwell.

Paine Falls

If you're traveling west along I-90 on your way to Cleveland, then Paine Falls is a must-see attraction. It's an excellent place to stop on a road trip to stretch your legs with a quick 0.10-mile walk from the parking lot to the falls. Don't forget to stop for snacks because there's more than enough room for a picnic.

Paine Falls is roughly 3 miles from the freeway. It's a great escape when you need a change of scenery, especially during the fall when the leaves start to change. The foliage turns the quiet metropark into a natural paradise from September to November.

The path to Paine Falls and the overlook is accessible for everyone, and the hike is easy for young families. You'll spend more time taking pictures than you do on the trek to and from the falls.

Best Time to Visit: The falls are at their strongest in the spring, but the best time to visit is October for the changing colors of the foliage.

Pass/Permit/Fees: The falls are free to visit.

Closest City or Town: Thompson

Physical Address: 5570 Paine Rd, Painesville, OH 44077

GPS Coordinates: 41.7178° N, 81.1441° W

Did You Know? The falls were previously known as Bakers Falls until 1974.

Art Tatum Celebration Column

Located in the heart of downtown Toledo, the Celebration Column was built to memorialize Art Tatum, one of the most legendary jazz musicians.

Art was born in Toledo to a music-loving family, and while his partial blindness made learning music more difficult, it didn't stop him from becoming one of the best piano players in the world.

The 27-foot column is designed to look like piano keys, spiraling in a pattern of glass and stainless steel and glowing after hours when the sun goes down. It's located right outside the Huntington Center, so everyone has access to it.

Best Time to Visit: Stop and see the statue late in the morning to avoid the crowds and grab lunch in downtown Toledo.

Pass/Permit/Fees: It is free to see the statue.

Closest City or Town: Toledo

Physical Address: Parking, 315N N St Clair St, Toledo, OH 43604. The column is on Madison Avenue.

GPS Coordinates: 41.6517° N, 83.5381° W

Did You Know? Art Tatum was known to have perfect pitch: the ability to identify and recreate musical notes without reference.

Maumee Bay State Park

Maumee Bay State Park is a favorite for swimmers and boaters. The park boasts access to Lake Erie and its own inland lake, along with boat ramps, boat rentals, and sandy beaches. If you'd rather fish on the water, Maumee is known as the "walleye capital of the world," and you're allowed to catch and keep up to six per Ohio law.

Visitors can see even more wildlife at the Trautman Nature Center, with its interactive displays and viewing windows. If exploration is your thing, hit one or all of the four trails in the park. Mouse Trail (2.5 miles) is the official hiking trail through the park, and the Interpretative Boardwalk hiking trail (2 miles) is ADA accessible. Take a jog on the paved Inland Lake trail (3 miles) along the water, or bring your bike for a ride on the Multi-Use Trail (2.5 miles).

Best Time to Visit: The best time to fish and hike is from July through November.

Pass/Permit/Fees: It's free to visit the park, and campsites start at $19 per day.

Closest City or Town: Toledo

Physical Address: 1400 State Park Rd, Oregon, OH 43616

GPS Coordinates: 41.6798° N, 83.3742° W

Did You Know? The swimming pool in the park is shaped like a heart.

Neil Armstrong First Flight Memorial

Neil Armstrong's memorial features a scale replica of the lunar module that took Armstrong and Buzz Aldrin to the surface of the moon, but it isn't immortalizing that first space flight. This is the site of Neil Armstrong's first flight *ever*.

When he was just six years old, Armstrong boarded his very first plane with his father at Warren Airfield. The airfield no longer exists, but this memorial captures a moment in time that defined modern history.

The memorial's lunar module stands 13 feet tall and 12 feet wide on a re-creation of the moon's surface, complete with the astronauts' footprints. The memorial was designed and built by steelworkers from the Trumbull Career and Technical Center.

Best Time to Visit: The best time to visit is weekday mornings around 11 a.m. when traffic is light.

Pass/Permit/Fees: It's free to visit the memorial.

Closest City or Town: Warren

Physical Address: 2553 Parkman Rd NW, Warren, OH 44485

GPS Coordinates: 41.2514° N, 80.8547° W

Did You Know? While young Neil was inspired by that flight, his father got nauseous on the tri-motor plane.

Horseshoe Falls

The hike to Horseshoe Falls is one of the easiest out-and-back trails in Ohio. It connects hikers to other trails in Caesar Creek State Park and can quickly change your short hike into an all-day affair if you wish. Start your hike from the parking lot and take the fork in the trail that leads down to the lake. Keep your eye out for fossils in the spillway. You'll reconnect with the rest of the trail from there and continue to the overlook above the falls. Follow the path to the suspension bridge over the stream, and keep left at the next fork to get a look at the waterfall from below.

The historical remnants of the grist mill that was once powered by the falls are just beyond Horseshoe Falls. You can then follow the trail back to the parking lot and drive on toward the visitor center to hop on the Perimeter Trailhead to nearby Crawdad Falls.

Best Time to Visit: The best time to see the falls is in April.

Pass/Permit/Fees: It's free to visit the falls, and campsites start at $29 per night.

Closest City or Town: Waynesville

Physical Address: 3286 N Clarksville Rd, Waynesville, OH 45068

GPS Coordinates: 39.4921° N, 84.0501° W

Did You Know? If you want to hunt for fossils at Horseshoe Falls, you can get free passes from the Caesar Creek State Park Visitors Center.

Crystal King and the Ohio Caverns

Ohio Caverns is the largest cave system in Ohio and home to Crystal King, the largest free-hanging stalactite in the state. Crystal King is 4 feet long and estimated to be over 200,000 years old. Year-round tours of the caverns take visitors to see Crystal King at the deepest point in the cave, but summer tours offer more opportunities to explore the rest of the cave. To reach the Crystal King, visitors must cross the Crystal Sea, an inch-deep reflection pool that sparkles from the crystals hanging above.

The Natural Bridge, a path carved by early excavators who were eager to protect the crystal columns, leads visitors into the Fantasy Land, to the Crystal King, and finally to the Good Luck Crystal. Many of the crystals hanging from the caverns' walls and ceilings are hundreds of thousands of years old and were discovered in 1897 by farmhands exploring a sinkhole.

Best Time to Visit: The caverns are open all year, but the best time to visit is between October and April.

Pass/Permit/Fees: Tours cost $10–$15 per child and $19–$29 per adult.

Closest City or Town: West Liberty

Physical Address: 2210 OH-245 E, West Liberty, OH 43357.

GPS Coordinates: 40.2376° N, 83.6967° W

Did You Know? Visitors are no longer allowed to touch the Good Luck Crystal.

Squire's Castle

Squire's Castle is actually the gatehouse to a castle that was never completed. It was commissioned in 1894 by Feargus B. Squire, who planned to turn the 525 acres into an English manor estate, but materials were hard to come by, and his wife never really liked the home. The Cleveland Park Board purchased the castle and preserved the area in what is now known as North Chagrin Reservation.

The original structure was three stories high, including a basement, but the interior structures have since been removed, and the lower levels filled in for safety. Hiking trails abound in the reservation, and the trail to Squire's Castle is a 3-mile loop. The trail is moderate with a steep incline at the beginning and end, but the remnants of the castle are open to explorers who reach it.

Best Time to Visit: The best time to visit Squire's Castle is between August and October.

Pass/Permit/Fees: It's free to explore the reservation.

Closest City or Town: Willoughby

Physical Address: 2844 River Rd, Willoughby Hills, OH 44094

GPS Coordinates: 41.5802° N, 81.4193° W

Did You Know? Some claim that Squire's late wife haunts the gatehouse, but she didn't die on the property and was rarely seen visiting it while she was alive.

Vasehenge

This quirky memorial commemorates Zanesville's history as the pottery capital of the country. The most famous pottery company in Zanesville was Weller Pottery, and the vases in Vasehenge were modeled after the company's original design.

Each vase stands higher than the average human, and they are painted with designs unique to the individual artists who made them.

In all, over 100 vases were created as part of a community-wide project in the mid-2000s. Various vases are scattered around town, but this is the only area where 18 are distinctively arranged in the Stonehenge pattern.

Best Time to Visit: The best time to see Vasehenge is in the spring.

Pass/Permit/Fees: It is free to visit Vasehenge.

Closest City or Town: Zanesville

Physical Address: Muskingum River Y Bridge, 732 Main St, Zanesville, OH 43701

GPS Coordinates: 39.9394° N, 82.0155° W

Did You Know? The original Weller Pottery factory in Zanesville was located on Pierce Street, five minutes away from Vasehenge.

Proper Planning

With this guide, you are well on your way to properly planning a marvelous adventure. When you plan your travels, you should become familiar with the area, save any maps to your phone for access without internet, and bring plenty of water—especially during the summer months. Depending on which adventure you choose, you will also want to bring snacks or even a lunch. For younger children, you should do your research and find destinations that best suit your family's needs. You should also plan when and where to get gas, local lodgings, and food. We've done our best to group these destinations based on nearby towns and cities to help make planning easier.

Dangerous Wildlife

There are several dangerous animals and insects you may encounter while hiking. With a good dose of caution and awareness, you can explore safely. Here are steps you can take to keep yourself and your loved ones safe from dangerous flora and fauna while exploring:

- Keep to the established trails.
- Do not look under rocks, leaves, or sticks.
- Keep hands and feet out of small crawl spaces, bushes, covered areas, or crevices.
- Wear long sleeves and pants to keep arms and legs protected.
- Keep your distance should you encounter any dangerous wildlife or plants.

Limited Cell Service

Do not rely on cell service for navigation or emergencies. Always have a map with you and let someone know where you are and how long you intend to be gone, just in case.

First Aid Information

Always travel with a first aid kit in case of emergencies.

Here are items you should be certain to include in your primary first aid kit:

- Nitrile gloves
- Blister care products
- Band-Aids in multiple sizes and waterproof type
- Ace wrap and athletic tape
- Alcohol wipes and antibiotic ointment
- Irrigation syringe
- Tweezers, nail clippers, trauma shears, safety pins
- Small zip-lock bags containing contaminated trash

It is recommended to also keep a secondary first aid kit, especially when hiking, for more serious injuries or medical emergencies. Items in this should include:

- Blood clotting sponges
- Sterile gauze pads
- Trauma pads
- Second-skin/burn treatment
- Triangular bandages/sling
- Butterfly strips
- Tincture of benzoin

- Medications (ibuprofen, acetaminophen, antihistamine, aspirin, etc.)
- Thermometer
- CPR mask
- Wilderness medicine handbook
- Antivenin

There is much more to explore, but this is a great start.

For information on all national parks, visit https://www.nps.gov/index.htm .

This site will give you information on up-to-date entrance fees and how to purchase a park pass for unlimited access to national and state parks. This site will also introduce you to all of the trails at each park.

Always check before you travel to destinations to make sure there are no closures. Some hiking trails close when there is heavy rain or snow in the area and other parks close parts of their land for the migration of wildlife. Attractions may change their hours or temporarily shut down for various reasons. Check the websites for the most up-to-date information.

Made in the USA
Columbia, SC
12 July 2024

38546263R00076